AF560369

Education and Inclusive Development in India

Education and Inclusive Development in India

Edited by

L.N. DASH
Reader in Economics
North Orissa University
Takatpur, Baripada, Orissa

REGAL PUBLICATIONS
New Delhi - 110 027

EDUCATION AND INCLUSIVE DEVELOPMENT IN INDIA

ISBN 978-81-8484-053-7

Typeset by
RAHUL COMPOSERS
358, Pocket-B, Phase-II, Sector-16 B, Dwarka, New Delhi - 110 075

Printed in India at
MAYUR ENTERPRISES
WZ Plot No. 3, Gujjar Market, Tihar Village, New Delhi - 110 018

Published by
REGAL PUBLICATIONS
F-159, Rajouri Garden, New Delhi - 110 027 • Phone : 45546396
E-mail : regalbookspub@yahoo.com

Contents

List of Contributors

Dr. L.N. Dash, Reader in Economics, North Orissa University, Baripada (Orissa).

Dr. N. Jaganathan, Reader in Economics, C.B.M. College, Coimbatore (Tamil Nadu).

Dr. Alka Samra, 21, Ashirwad Nagar, Roop Sagar Road, Udaipur (Rajasthan).

Dr. Kuldeep Kaur, Reader in Economics, Punjab School of Economics, Guru Nanak Dev University, Amritsar (Punjab).

Dr. Sailabala Debi, CMDR, Dharwad.

E. Nand Kumar, Research Scholar, Department of Economics, PSG College of Arts and Science, Civil Aerodrome Post, Coimbatore (Tamil Nadu).

Dr. A. Sangamithra, Lecturer in Economics, Bharathiar University, Coimbatore (Tamil Nadu).

Dr. Harvinder Kaur, Reader in Economics, Department of Correspondence Courses, Punjabi University, Patiala (Punjab).

Pradeep Kumar Choudhury, Research Scholar, NUEPA, New Delhi.

Manish Dev, Research Scholar, Department of Economics, Narain College, Ferozabad.

Dr. Sanjukta Das, Reader in Economics, Sambalpur University, Burla, Sambalpur (Orissa).

Dr. Kishor C. Samal, Professor of Economics, IGNOU, New Delhi.

Dr. Nighat Ahmad, Reader in Economics, Aligarh Muslim University, Aligarh (U.P.).

Dr. D.G. Mannivannan, Nopany Institute of Management, Kolkata.

Dr. Shaikh Saleem, Director, Millennium Institute of Management, Aurangabad.

Dr. Vidya Gawal, Lecturer, Millennium Institute of Management, Aurangabad.

Introduction

L.N. DASH

In the post-liberalisation period India has experienced expansion of unprecedented dimension. Despite this a number of divides and deficiencies have been spotted in various sectors of the economy. The growth has been termed as exclusionary in nature. Many economists and world organizations have dubbed it as jobless growth, voiceless growth, rootless growth, ruthless growth, and so on. No doubt, the economy is booming, but with gaps in it. The rapid economic development in the country has failed to take along with it various sectors and different sections of the people. Therefore, the vibrant economic growth will not be inclusive in nature. An inclusive growth can only bridge regional disparity, gender gap, the hiatus between the SCs and STs and other categories of people, the difference between the poor and the non-poor and so on. Of course, all efforts have been made to make development reach all sections of the society. Ever since the First Five Year Plan was implemented in 1951, growth and equity have been the twin objectives of planning strategy. But the gaps, instead of shrinking, have widened. Therefore, there has been change in thrust in the Tenth and Eleventh Plans. They aim at faster, more broad-based and inclusive growth in the Indian economy in order to reduce poverty and bridge the various divides that continues to fragment the society. But the means to achieve the goals have been changed. Education has been identified as the weapon to achieve the goals. Therefore, there has been a U-turn in the emphasis laid down on the education sector to achieve the development goals. It has been realized, of late, that inclusive development can only be achieved by inclusive education. India's young demographic bulge—with more than half of its population aged 25 or younger—can speedily turn into a liability if human resources are not managed effectively. Both growth and equity are endangered in the absence of better education. Education is supposed to be the first step in nation-building. Owing to this the Eleventh Plan has accorded top priority to education. The 86th Constitutional amendment making free and compulsory education for children of 6-14 age group a fundamental right is a milestone in the development of education in India. Despite all this the education sector is fraught with problems which need serious attention.

Notwithstanding the goal of universalisation of primary education in India, 59 million children are not attending school. India already has one of the highest pupil-teacher ratio in Asia, according to Global Education Digest, 2005. India has a pupil-teacher ratio of 44 at the pre-primary level, which is the highest in Asia. The number decreases to 42 at the primary level. The gross enrolment ratio, which measures the number of students at a given level as a percentage of total population in the relevant age group, stands at 71 per cent at the lower secondary level and 39 per cent at the higher secondary level in India. Those are significantly lower than the world averages of 79 per cent and 51 per cent respectively. In terms of access to primary and secondary education girls are at a disadvantage in India. Only 47 per cent of the entrants at the primary level are females. This reduces to 43 per cent at the secondary level.

Elementary education is the foundation of the education pyramid which received a big push during the Tenth Plan through the Sarva Shiksha Abhiyan (SSA). The SSA has brought primary education to the doorsteps of millions of children. Despite this only 10.71 lakh (87 per cent) habitations had a primary school within a distance of 1 km and the number of uncovered habitations stood at 1.61 lakh (13 per cent), according to the Seventh Educational Survey (2002). The number of primary schools in the country increased from 6.64 lakh in 2001-02 to 7.68 lakh in 2004-05. During the same period the number of upper primary schools increased from 2.20 lakh to 2.75 lakh. The decision to add an additional 2.23 lakh primary and upper primary schools, 1.88 lakh new classrooms has led to the increase of enrolment at elementary education level from 159 million in 2001-02 to 182 million in 2004-05. But the social and gender disparity that exist at primary and upper primary education level needs to be tackled, particularly in the states of Bihar, Rajasthan, Jharkhand, Madhya Pradesh, Uttar Pradesh and Gujarat.

The SSA has brought down the number of school drop-outs from 32 million in 2001-02 to 7 million in 2006-07 (Figure 1). It has been found that 48 districts in 10 states accounted for over 50,000 out-of-school children. The number of such districts came down to 29 in 2005-06. About 6.9 per cent of the total children in the 6-13 age group were out of school, a bulk of whom are from the poorer sections of rural households.

FIG. 1
Out of School Children (in crore)

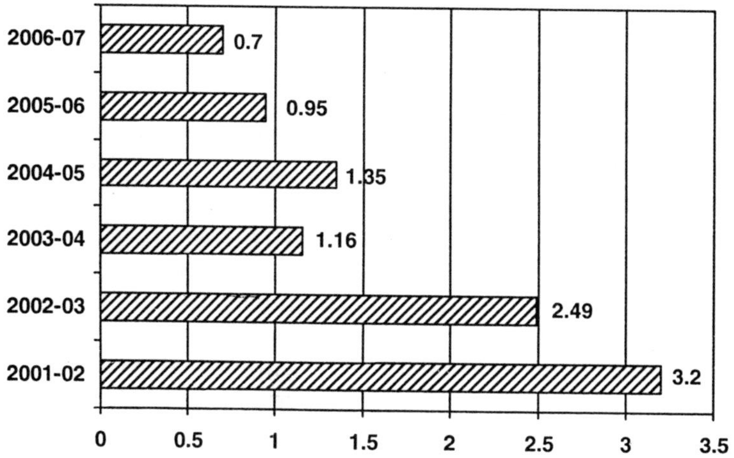

The success of the SSA in achieving large scale enrolment of children has thrown a challenge to secondary education. It serves as a bridge between elementary and higher education.

The population of children in the age group of 14-18 years is estimated to be 119.7 million in 2006, whereas the enrolment in secondary education is about 37 million in 2004-05. There are glaring inter-state and intra-state variations in enrolment, drop-outs and access to secondary education. At the national level, the average number of secondary and higher secondary schools per 1 lakh population is as low as 14. However, it is lower than the national average in Bihar (4), Uttar Pradesh (7), West Bengal (10), Jharkhand (4) and Chhattisgarh (12). In addition to this, the number of secondary and higher secondary schools per 100 sq. km is only 4. The figures in Bihar, Uttar Pradesh, Rajasthan, Madhya Pradesh, Chhattisgarh and Jharkhand fall below the national average. Nearly 60 per cent of secondary schools are with private management. The GER for SCs and STs at secondary education level is 45.4 per cent and 37.2 per cent respectively as compared to the overall GER of 51.6 per cent. The GER for girls belonging to these categories of children is 37.6 per cent and 30.5 per cent respectively, indicating a substantial gender gap in enrolment for these groups.

The absence of infrastructure facilities in schools, non-availability of quality teachers, etc. pose serious problem in the expansion of school education in the country. The delivery of quality education is possible only through quality teachers. There is an urgent need that every school should have basic amenities such as good buildings with library, laboratories, safe drinking water facility, clean toilets, play ground, etc. Education is supposed to be the first step in nation-building. But India simply does not have enough teachers to impart teaching. The country already faces a shortage of 8 lakh teachers in primary and middle schools. And the situation is going to get even worse in the days to come. The recommended pupil-teacher ratio for primary classes is one teacher for 40 students—though in advanced countries like the US or UK, and even in China, this ratio is already below 30. However, even going by the ratio of 1:40, India needs 60 lakh teachers for classes I-VIII, and has only 52 lakh—a figure which is set to shrink further. The pupil-teacher ratio improves for higher classes. It is 1:33 for classes IX to XII, and 1:25 in higher education. But this is because many students drop out. Assuming all persons in the age group 15-19 were to start attending school, India would need about 38 lakh teachers for classes IX to XII at a pupil-taecher ratio of 1:30 for higher classes. It has just 26 lakh teachers, a 12 lakh shortage. All this is possible only by earmarking an additional 2 to 3 per cent of GDP.

The higher education in India has witnessed many-fold increase in institutional capacity since 1950. In 1950 there were only 25 universities which have gone up to 431 in 2008. (Table 1). The number of colleges has increased from 700 to 20,677 and the number of teachers from 15,000 to 5.05 lakhs. All these have given rise to increase in student enrolment from one lakh to 116.12 during 1950 to 2008. The access to higher education is measured in terms of gross enrolment ratio (GER). The GER in the age group of 18 to 23 years increased from 0.7 per cent in 1950-51 to 1.4 per cent in 1960-61. In 2006-07, it went up to 11 per cent. However, there is regional variation in GER. As against the 11 per cent all India average, the GER is lower in states of Arunachal Pradesh, Bihar, Meghalaya, Mizoram, Rajasthan, Sikkim, Tripura and Jharkhand. There are also large number of districts with lower GER. Out of 584 total districts in the country, 373 districts had GER lower than the national average. Therefore, the Eleventh Plan has recognized the dual problem of low enrolment rate and regional imbalance. Further, the 11 per cent enrolment rate at the national level is too low compared to 23 per cent of world average and 55 per cent for developed countries. We are in India talking of sustainable growth. And a sustained economic growth requires a minimum of 20 per cent to 25 per cent enrolment in higher education.

TABLE 1

Institutional Capacity in Higher Education

Sl. No.	*Institutional capacity indicator*	*1950*	*2008*
1.	No. of university level institutions (including 11 private universities)	25	431
2.	No. of colleges	700	20,677
3.	No. of teachers	15,000	5.05 lakh
4.	No. of students enrolled	1 lakh	116.12 lakh

There is, therefore, the objective to raise GER to 15 per cent by 2012 and to 21 per cent by the end of Twelfth Plan. In absolute number it would mean an increase of about 7 million students by 2012.

Although the enrolment rate in higher education is about 11 per cent, there are significant inter-group disparities in access to higher education. The NSS data for 2004-05 show that there are rural-urban disparities. The enrolment rate is 6.70 per cent and 19.90 per cent for the rural and urban areas respectively. In other words, the GER in the urban areas is three times higher compared to rural areas. There are also inter-caste/tribe disparities. The GER among the SCs (6.57 per cent), the STs (6.52 per cent), and the OBCs (8.77 per cent) was much lower than others (17.22 per cent). The disparities are also noticed between religious groups. The GER for the Hindus, Muslims, the Christians, the Sikhs and others stood at 11.9, 6.84, 16.68, 12.0 and 15.4 percentages respectively. Thus, the GER was the lowest among the Muslims followed by the Hindus. There is also

TABLE 2
Disparities in GER in Higher Education, 2004-05

Disparities	*GER*
Area	
(i) Rural	6.70
(ii) Urban	19.90
Gender	
(i) Male	12.40
(ii) Female	9.10
Social	
(i) SCs	6.57
(ii) STs	6.52
(iii) OBCs	8.77
(iv) Others	17.22
All	11.00

Source : Government of India, *Tenth Five Year Plan*, Vol. II, New Delhi, Government of India, Planning Commission.

gender disparity in GER in higher education—the GER being 12.40 per cent for males and 9.10 per cent for the females. In addition to this, the GER among SC, ST and OBC females is lower. (Table 2) With high disparities inclusive education for inclusive development may not be within reach in the near future.

1

Education and the Knowledge Economy of India

L.N. DASH

Education plays a key role in accelerating the knowledge economy. The role of the highly educated and skilled people is vital in creating, sharing, disseminating and using knowledge effectively. The 'knowledge workers' and the 'knowledge technologists' are at the centre of the knowledge economy. Knowledge workers refer to the doctors, lawyers, teachers, engineers and the accountants. On the contrary, the knowledge technologists include the computer technicians, software designers, manufacturing technologists, etc. During the coming years these knowledge technologists will be a powerful social group. The development of a knowledge economy requires a flexible education system. Development of basic education marks the beginning of such a system. Basic education provides the foundation for learning, continues with secondary and tertiary education and ultimately develops the core of education. Then it extends into a system of life-long learning. A life-long learning system extends from early childhood to retirement which includes both formal training in schools, training institutions and universities. It also includes non-formal learning on the job and from people in the community. No doubt, a large number of people are making their mark in India and abroad in the field of science and engineering, IT and R&D, but they are only a small fraction of India's population. India, in order to become a knowledge economy, has to develop its human capital base and create knowledge workers. In this way they can contribute to India's growth, development and competitiveness in the global economy. It is high time that India should make its education system attuned to the characteristics of the global environment. During the last couple of years India has improved marginally in the field of education. Now it is ahead of other countries in South Asia and Africa region, but lags behind Brazil and China. India also trails behind the countries like Poland, Russia and Korea who have progressed significantly in tertiary education. Although India has made some progress in literacy rate, its average years of schooling stands at 5.06 years which is higher than Brazil (4.88 years) but lower than that of China (6.35 years). Countries like Poland (9.84 years), Russia (10.03 years), and Korea (10.84 years) are far ahead of India in this regard. The picture is not better in case of secondary and tertiary enrolments in which India lags behind many of its comparator countries. However, merely scoring better on the above aspects will not help our country to perform better in the knowledge economy. A transition to the knowledge economy can be made only if its people can create, share and use knowledge effectively. Reform in India's educational system should be brought about to achieve higher participation, equity and quality not only at the school level but also at the higher education level.

It is here pertinent to highlight some of the important trends in education and human resource development in India and some important issues relating to strengthening India's educational system. It is seen that literacy rate in India has risen considerably during the last decade. It has increased from 52.2 per cent in 1991 to 65.4 per cent in 2001. The male literacy rate is 75.9 per cent which was 56 per cent in 1981. As compared to this 54.2 per cent of the women were literate in 2001 which was

30 per cent in 1981. The gap between male and female literacy has come down from 28.8 per cent in 1981 to 21.7 per cent in 2001. In spite of the impressive improvement in India's literacy rate, regional variations exist. To cite an example, Kerala has a literacy rate of 91 per cent while the literacy rate in Bihar is limited to only 48 per cent. There are constraints in reducing adult illiteracy. Moreover, a strong basic education system is a necessary pre-condition to enhance the efficiency of the Indian economy. Higher investments in basic education will increase the supply of manpower and enhance the quality of labour force. They are needed for making higher economic development in the country. Table shows that enrollment of students at all levels—primary, secondary, and tertiary—has increased in India. The enrollment rate in primary schools has gone up in the past decade, from 97 per cent in 1990 to 99 per cent in 2001. The rate in case of secondary school went up from 44 per cent in 1990 to 50 per cent in 2001. These figures, however, are lower than China (67 per cent in 2001) and Brazil. Despite India's achievement, the total out-of-school children in India accounts for one-quarter of the world's 104 million out-of-school children. Among the various factors, wide-spread teacher vacancies, teacher absenteeism, high drop-out rates, inadequate teaching and learning materials, etc. are important. The participation of girls of 6-14 year age group in elementary education is far from satisfactory. Table 1.1 presents the per student expenditure pattern of primary, secondary and tertiary education in selected countries. In India, the expenditure composition is skewed towards secondary and tertiary education. At the primary level public expenditure is $ 7.2 which increases to $ 23.01 and $ 92.5 at the secondary and tertiary levels. The picture is different in case of Korea. The per student public expenditure goes on diminishing from $ 14 at the primary level to $ 17.9 and $ 7.37 at the secondary and tertiary levels respectively. Tertiary education, of course, is expensive. Keeping in view the GDP level of India, more private investment should be encouraged in the higher education level and more public investment should be made for primary and secondary education. This will help to strengthen the human resource base and needs of the knowledge economy.

TABLE 1.1
Education Spending in India and Comparator Countries

(in dollars)

Country	*GDP Per capita*	*Public expenditure per student*		
		Primary education	*Secondary education*	*Tertiary education*
Pakistan	420	n.a.	n.a.	n.a.
India	460	7.2	23.01	92.5
Indonesia	690	3.2	8.7	12.2
China	890	6.1	12.1	85.8
Russia	1750	n.a.	20.5	15.8
Thailand	1940	12:5	12.8	38.2
South Korea	2820	14	17.9	7.37
Brazil	3070	12.5	12.6	72.8
Malaysia	3330	11.2	19.9	86.1
Mexico	5530	11.7	13.8	45.2

n.a. : Not available.
Source : Gopalji and Suman Bhakri, *Statistical Data on Indian Economy* (New Delhi: Taxmann Allied Services, 2005), p. 186.

Tertiary education, nevertheless, is critical for developing the knowledge economies. India has 431 universities, 18,064 colleges, many other world class institutions like the IITs, IIMs, Indian Institute of Science and 17 Regional Engineering Colleges (later upgraded to National Institute of Technologies). In 2001, the gross enrollment ratio (GER) for tertiary education in India was 11.4 per cent compared with 12.7 per cent for China, 59 per cent for Poland and 82 per cent for Korea. Of late, there has been mushrooming of tertiary education institutions in India which has given rise to increase in enrollments. These institutions are mostly privately-owned and lack adequate academic and physical infrastructure, heavily controlled by government regulations, and subject to government interventions. At the university level, the universities lack autonomy in management and academic affairs, fee level, and so on. Furthermore, the poor remuneration and infrastructure in most of the tertiary educational institutions fail to attract or retain high quality faculty members. Many of them also face faculty shortages. Enhancement of not only quality but also the relevance of tertiary education is pertinent. This is because about 9.3 per cent students in India are pursuing undergraduate degrees and 85 per cent of them receive general degrees who cannot be effective knowledge workers. The degrees received by a large number of students are not marketable. Therefore, the 'clubbed education' plan adopted by the government, of late, is a welcome step in this regard. The system will not only enable the students to receive a general degree, but also a utility-oriented degree *pari pasu*. The plan would only increase the duration of undergraduate course from three to four years. The other way of improving quality is to foster partnership among Indian universities and Indian universities with foreign ones. This would enable optimal utilisation of existing resources. The efficiency of the faculty can improve through entrepreneur exchange programmes. The Indian School of Business in Hyderabad, for example, has developed such partnership with two high standard business schools in the United States (The Kellogg School of Management and Wharton School) and with London Business School in the United Kingdom. The Indian Institute of Management (IIMs) are also increasingly focusing on foreign research tie-ups with reputed foreign universities. The IIM at Ahmedabad, Bangalore and Lucknow are in the process of entering research partnership with global B-Schools. Close on the heels of a research tie-up is between IIM, Calcutta and Yale School of Management and the IIM, Ahmedabad is in talks with international B-schools like University of Amsterdam and Duke University for research. The IIM, Lucknow is also exploring possible research links with five B-schools in the United States, Europe and France. The IIM, Bangalore is in talks with four foreign B-schools for possible collaborations in areas of marketing and financing. Research tie-ups are important for cross-culture learning and help the institutes in the era of globalization. Research collaborations also add to the international reputation of the institute and the faculty. This gives an opportunity for the students to gain internationally recognized credentials.

During the last couple of years it has been seen that many foreign universities have started their companies in India. These opportunities enable the students to receive high quality education and externally recognized credentials. This has two beneficial effects. First, such competition is likely to enhance the quality of tertiary education in the indigenous institutions imparting tertiary education. Secondly, it provides scope to export its tertiary education and to attract large number of well-paying foreign students to our country.

In the field of science and technology education a few points need to be brought to the fore. India has one of the world's largest systems of post-secondary science and engineering education. Consequently, the country has largest stocks of scientists, engineers, and technicians in the world. Despite this, deficiencies are found in India's scientific and manpower development system which warrants to be corrected at the earliest in order to realize the huge potential for economic prosperity. Some of them are the lack of autonomy, accountability, little authority on faculty appointments and student admissions, structure and contents of programmes, evaluation of student performance, financial management, etc. Many of them lack physical infrastructure and technology. The libraries need to be interlinked to achieve higher student performance. Besides, the reputed world-class IITs, IIMs and Indian Institute of Science, there are large number of newly-established engineering colleges which do not meet the minimum quality standards. The status of education in these engineering colleges is poor. Most of the colleges do not have faculty. The total number of seats in about 1450 colleges comes to 495,000. Out of this available pool, only 225,000 graduates have the requisite training to be employed by IT firms. Therefore, the professional workforce coming out of these institutions does not find suitable employment due to a yawning gap between knowledge and job opportunities in professional field. Many of the pass-outs are able to get some job opportunities with low salaries.

A large number of science and technology personnel leave the country to find better opportunities abroad. The extent of international mobility of Indian students can be fathomed from the fact that only 15,000 Indians left for the United States in 1990 which increased to 50,000 in 2000. Nearly 80 per cent of the Indian students who enrolled in different OECD countries in 2001 went to the United States. In 1999, 165,000 Indian residents in the United States had science and engineering as their highest degree. Now the country is confronting the serious problem of outflow of tertiary educated workforce. The vast outflow of highly skilled health professional has posed a problem before the country. Nearly 49 per cent of graduates of the country's leading medical institute—All India Institute of Medical Sciences (AIIMS)—emigrated during the 1990s. Their migration means that public resources have subsidized high-level human capital formation in other developed countries. According to the estimates of the *Human Development Report-2001* India incurred a loss of resources to the tune of $ 2 billion a year due to emigration of computer professionals to the United States alone. Each year about 100,000 Indians are expected to immigrate to the United States while India invests between $ 15,000 and $ 20,000 in educating each of them.

Notwithstanding all these, India has many positive aspects in educational system. Necessary reforms could be undertaken so that it can significantly contribute to its knowledge economy. The measures to strengthen education and human resources include enhancing basic education, overhauling tertiary education, rectifying weaknesses in science and technology education, promoting policy and institutional reforms for scientific research and development, strengthening skill development and training, encouraging life-long learning, involving the private sector in education, training and human resource development. In a competitive global market, skills matter more than ever. In India, the vast majority of the people are unskilled and uneducated. The capabilities of these people must be enhanced in order to make the economy more vibrating. Not under-emphasising secondary and tertiary education, the government should take steps to improve the skill and education levels of the mass of people through primary and vocational education. China has been able to achieve high growth rate because of its workforce that has a basic education. In 1980, China had 66 per cent of its population with schooling as compared to 34 per cent in India. With regard to average educational attainment level, India had 5.06 years as compared to 6.35 years in China in 2000. During the last two decades, the share of population who completed primary education has almost doubled, from 4.7 per cent to 10.5 per cent. In China, the same increased from 9.9 per cent in 1980 to 14.8 per cent in 2000. At the present level of population increase in India, the country will continue to have a large young population. They can effectively participate in the knowledge economy if they can be extended secondary education and provided skills. It is not only urgent to provide basic education, but also vital for the nation to provide secondary and tertiary education to the large mass of people in order to make them effective partner in development.

Indian tertiary education system needs to become more demand-driven, quality conscious and forward looking. There is also a need to bring about a systematic education reform in science and technology. It includes empowerment of the institutions with accountability, optimal utilisation of resources, networking of institutions for capacity enhancement, improving quality and promotion of excellence, establishing linkage with community and industry, and so on. Several reform measures, however, have been taken in these regard. During the Tenth Five-Year Plan the government has upgraded many science and engineering colleges for quality improvement. Many of the state engineering colleges have been provided greater autonomy. In future, they can become important players in the higher education market. Many more steps need to be taken for quality education. A number of policy and institutional reforms also are to be taken to produce high quality scientists and technologists to meet the country's demand for scientific research and development. Technology is changing fast. There is, therefore, a need for the enterprises to invest in workers' training to remain competitive. If the initial education of the workers is high, the cost of imparting new skills becomes less. India should focus on this aspect to keep its workers globally competitive.

The importance of knowledge and innovation in economies is increasing. Therefore, the education and training system should evolve into life-long training system. People should have access to learning system on an on-going basis. China has recognized its importance and started providing massive training to its labour force. It is also important for India to face the challenges in the same way. It is not possible for the government to undertake the all-round changes in the education system of India. The private sector has to play an active role in improving the quality and quantity of education.

2

Education and Economic Development in India

N. JAGANATHAN

Economic development is a process whereby the real per capita income of a country increases over a long period of time. The increase in the quality of human beings by education, health, nutrition, etc. helps to increase the physical output. Therefore, human resource development along with physical capital formation plays a useful role in economic development. The human resources can be developed by providing formal education from elementary to the higher level, technical and professional, on-the-job training, adult education programmes, and correspondence or distance education. Although mass education is an essential input, the quality and level of literacy also matter substantially for development. All concerned with education know that the human resources of a nation can be developed by making investments in education of the order commensurate with the nature and dimension of the task. The provision of educational expenditure is important under the state activities for economic development.

Throughout the history of independent India, the Indian government has strived to work for educational development and thereby to increase productivity in order to accelerate the pace of economic development. A lot has been achieved in the past five decades. Hence, an attempt is made in this study to anlayse educational development and the relationship between educational development and economic development. The overall objective of the study is to anlayse the relationship between educational development and economic development in India.

OBJECTIVES

The specific objectives of the study are :

(1) to study the size, composition, and growth of educational expenditure;
(2) to study the growth of educational infrastructure facilities and attainments; and
(3) to study the inter-relationship between educational development and economic development.

METHODOLOGY

Sources of Data

Secondary data were collected for Gross Domestic Product at factor cost, population, wholesale price index, educational expenditure and its components, educational institutions, teachers in schools, enrolment by levels of education, and literacy by age and sex from Indian Public Finance Statistics, Indian Economic Survey, Socio-Economic Indicators—India, Women and Men in India, Man Power Profile—India Year Book, and Educational Statistics at a Glance.

Period of Study

Data regarding educational expenditure and its components, educational infrastructures and attainments and economic development were collected for 24 years, i.e., from 1981-82 to 2004-05. The total period was divided into two sub-periods, viz., 1981-82 to 1990-91 and 1991-92 to 2004-05 in order to make a comparative analysis between pre and post-New Economic Reform Policy periods.

Tools of Analyses

Secondary data were collected and the analytical tools such as percentage analysis, Chow test, growth analysis, test for difference between means, elasticity of educational expenditures, ADF test and Granger's causality test were used. Before calculating percentage values, the expenditure in current year value was converted to constant year value taking 1993-94 prices as the base year.

Scope and Limitation of the Study

This kind of study will unfold the involvement of central and state governments for the allocation of educational expenditure; exhibit the growth of educational infrastructure facilities and the attainments in them, and the relationship between educational development and economic development.

There is a need for increasing trend in educational expenditure by the governments and private sector. But the data for private sector educational expenditures are not available. Therefore, the study is limited to educational expenditure by the governments.

EMPIRICAL ANALYSIS

Growth of Educational Expenditure

Expenditure on education improves the knowledge and skill of the people. Hence, an attempt is made to anlayse the size, composition and growth of educational expenditure in this section. The major educational components are elementary, secondary and university education as shown in Table 2.1. The size of expenditure on elementary, secondary and university was Rs. 4598 crore, Rs. 3431 crore and Rs. 1853 crore in 1981-82, which increased to Rs. 11,727 crore, Rs. 8314 crore and Rs. 3697 crore in 1990-91 and Rs. 256.85 crore, Rs. 186.23 crore and Rs. 5426 crore in 2004-05. It shows that educational expenditure

TABLE 2.1
Educational Expenditure (Rs. 100 Crore)

Years	*Elementary*	*Secondary*	*Adults*	*Technical*	*University*	*Others*	*Total*
(1)	*(2)*	*(3)*	*(4)*	*(5)*	*(6)*	*(7)*	*(8)*
			Period-1				
1981-82	45.98	34.31	1.06	05.66	18.53	4.57	110.11
1982-83	55.37	38.96	1.32	06.57	20.11	4.90	127.24
1983-84	58.51	41.38	1.77	06.57	20.97	5.59	134.78
1984-85	60.10	43.23	1.13	07.41	22.85	6.62	141.34
1985-86	74.98	51.16	2.71	10.38	26.65	5.59	171.46
1986-87	79.95	55.78	3.00	10.82	29.69	6.54	185.78
1987-88	91.89	61.96	3.08	12.43	30.02	5.45	204.83
1988-89	99.82	72.70	4.09	12.28	36.33	6.09	231.32
1989-90	114.54	79.67	4.13	12.58	39.58	6.71	257.21
1990-91	117.27	83.14	4.92	13.12	36.97	6.17	261.59
Mean	79.84	56.23	2.72	9.78	28.17	5.82	182.57
C.V	31.69	31.21	50.60	29.88	26.99	12.54	030.07
C.G.R	11.21*	10.82*	19.29*	10.74*	09.27*	3.02#	10.59*

(Contd.)

TABLE 2.1 (Contd.)

(1)	(2)	(3)	(4)	(5)	(6)	(7)	(8)
			Period-2				
1991-92	113.65	82.45	3.61	12.47	34.66	5.75	252.59
1992-93	114.74	81.86	3.52	12.79	34.60	7.08	254.59
1993-94	120.82	83.58	4.39	13.49	33.82	11.56	267.65
1994-95	124.17	86.34	4.50	13.70	33.62	9.66	271.99
1995-96	133.70	94.43	5.02	14.61	34.88	6.54	289.18
1996-97	149.79	105.23	5.73	16.04	35.99	6.49	319.26
1997-98	161.57	111.85	6.50	18.51	38.74	6.97	344.14
1998-99	191.05	133.70	8.27	20.72	42.68	7.38	403.80
1999-00	225.31	159.16	10.30	23.74	45.81	7.70	472.02
2000-01	214.22	150.81	10.04	22.77	42.14	6.00	445.97
2001-02	221.65	163.52	10.55	24.15	46.15	6.85	472.87
2002-03	235.45	169.45	10.82	26.45	49.23	7.26	498.66
2003-04	242.36	178.45	11.05	27.15	51.24	9.45	519.70
2004-05	256.85	186.23	11.45	30.12	54.26	10.25	549.16

Mean	178.95	127.65	7.55	19.77	41.27	7.78	382.97
C.V	29.66	30.92	40.77	30.47	17.21	22.44	28.38
C.G.R	07.44*	07.70*	10.92*	07.59*	03.92*	00.94@	07.03*
t(m)	-05.45*	-05.33*	-04.62*	-04.83*	-04.23*	-03.33*	-05.34*

Note : C.G.R.—Compound growth rate.
C.V.—Coefficient of variation.

* Statistically significant at one per cent level.

\# Statistically significant at five per cent level.

@ Statistically not significant at five per cent level.

t (m)—'t' test values for the difference between means of two periods.

increased in both the periods. This uptrend was confirmed by larger mean values in period-2 than in period-1 for all the components of educational expenditure. The 't' test values for the difference between the mean values of period-1 and period-2 was statistically significant at one per cent level. The C.V value for most of the components was comparatively less in period-2 than in period-1, showing relatively less instability during the post-economic reform period.

The compound growth rate was less for all the components in period-2 than in period-1. It was again due to the reason that the base for the estimation of growth rate was larger in Period-2 than in Period-1. Hence, one could observe that there was an increasing trend in educational expenditure during the post-economic reform period in order to serve the increasing educational needs of the people. Therefore, the general inference was that the governments had allocated more funds for educational improvement during the post-economic reform period. There was more stable uptrend in education expenditure, even though the growth rate was comparatively smaller in period-2. Thus, it could be inferred that the uptrend in educational expenditure of governments during post-economic reform period had welfare implication. The estimated 'F' values of the different components of educational expenditure of combined, union and state governments for the Chow test are given in Table 2.2. It shows that all the estimated 'F' values are statistically significant. It indicates that there was a structural change or structural instability between Period-1 and Period-2 in the different components of educational expenditure for all the governments.

Elasticity of Educational Expenditure

In order to estimate the elasticity of the components of educational expenditure, a log-linear function (in $Y_t = \alpha_0 + \alpha_1$ in $X_t + u_t$) was used, with the assumptions of the Classical linear regression model. The dependent and independent variables are different components of educational expenditure (Y_t) and GDP (X_t).

The elasticity of educational expenditures with respect to GDP is presented in Table 2.3. The elasticity of total educational expenditure and its components was less in Period-2 than in

Period-1. Thus, the elasticity of educational expenditure with respect to GDP was relatively less for education during the post-economic reform period.

TABLE 2.2
Chow Test for Educational Expenditure

Sl. No.	Details	S_5 Value	S_4 Value	F Value
1.	Elementary	1815.37	3116.10	17.17*
2.	Secondary	1045.24	1967.33	18.82*
3.	Adult	8.12	17.59	21.66*
4.	Technical	22.43	60.68	27.05*
5.	University	90.73	166.96	18.40*
6.	Others	41.40	1.93	0.47@
	Total	7309.19	13589.46	18.59*

Note : S_1 = RSS_T S_2 = RSS_1 S_3 = RSS_2
$S_4 = (S_1 + S_2)$ $S_5 = (S_1 — S_4)$.
RSS—Residual sum of squares
* Statistically significant at one per cent level.
$ Statistically significant at five per cent level.
@ Statistically not significant at five per cent level

TABLE 2.3
Elasticity with Respect to GD (%)

Sl. No.	Details	Period-I	Period-II
1.	Elementary Education	1.91	1.33
2.	Secondary Education	1.87	1.30
3.	Adult Education	3.18	2.06
4.	Technical Education	1.80	1.26
5.	University Education	1.61	0.52
6.	Total	1.82	1.20

Note : All the values of the elasticity values are statistically significant at one per cent level.
I—Period-1 (1981-82 to 1990-91).
II—Period-2 (1991-92 to 2004-05).

EDUCATIONAL INFRASTRUCTURE AND ATTAINMENT

For an overall development of the economy, development of education is important. Hence, the effect of educational expenditure in terms of educational infrastructure development and educational attainment is discussed in this section. The number of schools per lakh population and teachers in schools per 10,000 students were taken as educational infrastructure development. Enrolment by level of education and male and female literacy rates were taken as educational attainment. The number of primary and secondary schools per lakh population was an indicator of educational infrastructure development and therefore the details are given in Table 2.4. It is seen that the number of primary schools per lakh population declined by six schools in Period-1 and by eight schools in Period-2. The fall was higher in Period-2. But the number of secondary schools per lakh population increased by 0.37 in Period-1 and by eight schools in Period-2. The mean value was significantly lesser for secondary schools and larger for primary schools in Period-2. The compound growth rate was negative for primary schools and positive for secondary schools, but the negative growth rate was relatively lesser in Period-2. The C.V. was relatively smaller

TABLE 2.4
Number of Schools per Lakh Population

Years	*Primary Schools*	*Secondary Schools*
(1)	*(2)*	*(3)*
	Period-1	
1981-82	72.80	17.68
1982-83	71.15	17.42
1983-84	70.42	17.48
1984-85	70.32	17.57
1985-86	70.05	17.86
1986-87	68.84	17.90
1987-88	68.40	18.09

(Contd.)

TABLE 2.4 (Contd.)

(1)	*(2)*	*(3)*
1988-89	67.41	17.98
1989-90	66.68	17.90
1990-91	66.86	18.05
Mean	69.29	17.79
C.V	02.88	01.35
C.G.R	-00.93*	00.37*
	Period-2	
1991-92	66.21	18.22
1992-93	65.51	18.18
1993-94	63.95	18.25
1994-95	64.48	18.55
1995-96	63.95	18.77
1996-97	63.81	19.06
1997-98	64.23	19.29
1998-99	63.76	19.35
1999-2000	64.11	19.78
2000-01	62.68	20.24
2001-02	61.56	21.26
2002-03	60.25	23.15
2003-04	59.46	25.56
2004-05	58.21	26.48
Mean	65.62	19.34
C.V	05.82	12.67
C.G.R	-00.80@	01.36*
t(m)	03.06*	-2.35*

Note : C.G.R.—Compound growth rate.
C.V.— Coefficient of variation.
* Significant at one per cent level.
@ Significant at five per cent level.
t (m) — 't' test values for difference between means of two periods.

for primary schools and larger for secondary schools in Period-2 compared to Period-1. Therefore, the number of primary schools declined at a lesser rate and secondary schools per lakh population was at a higher rate during the post-economic reform period. The inference is that the number of primary schools had increased slower than the population and that was inconsistent with the goals of universal education and 100 per cent enrolment. Addition in investment by the governments and encouragement of private investment in primary schools should be the policy. It would call for further increase in secondary schools of to discourage drop-out at that level. The number of teachers in primary and secondary schools per 10,000 students was taken as another indicator of educational infrastructure. It is shown in Table 2.5.

TABLE 2.5
Teachers in Schools Per 10,000 Students

Years	*Primary Schools*	*Secondary Schools*
(1)	*(2)*	*(3)*
	Period-1	
1981-82	189.73	438.92
1982-83	179.05	381.32
1983-84	174.92	355.58
1984-85	173.44	354.60
1985-86	171.17	354.58
1986-87	172.33	363.21
1987-88	170.44	352.48
1988-89	170.36	347.14
1989-90	169.43	339.05
1990-91	166.02	315.59
Mean	173.69	360.25
C.V	03.81	08.97
C.G.R	-01.06*	-02.34*

(Contd.)

TABLE 2.5 (Contd.)

(1)	(2)	(3)
	Period-2	
1991-92	162.93	303.09
1992-93	165.76	318.18
1993-94	167.32	331.09
1994-95	160.61	317.58
1995-96	161.90	317.87
1996-97	162.20	314.96
1997-98	165.28	313.16
1998-99	171.69	317.12
1999-2000	168.93	308.31
2000-01	166.61	309.81
2001-02	169.45	311.26
2002-03	172.23	312.45
2003-04	174.23	314.23
2004-05	177.45	316.75
Mean	167.61	314.70
C.V	02.99	02.03
C.G.R	00.57*	-0.09@
t(m)	02.56*	05.18*

Note : C.G.R—Compound growth rate.
C.V—Coefficient of variation.
* Significant at one per cent level.
@ Not significant at five per cent level.
t (m) 't' test values for difference between means of two periods.

It could be seen that the number of teachers per 10,000 students in primary schools declined in Period-1 from 190 teachers in 1981-82 to 166 teachers in 1990-91. But in Period-2, the number of primary school teachers increased from 163 to 177, i.e., by 15. It increased relatively more in Period-2 than in Period-1. In the secondary schools also the number of teachers per 10,000 students declined from 439 in 1981-82 to 316 in 1990-

91, i.e., by 123 teachers per 10,000 students. In Period-2, there was a marginal increase by 14 teachers per lakh population. The mean value for teachers in primary and secondary schools was significantly less in Period-2. The negative growth rate of teachers in primary schools in Period-1 became positive in Period-2. The negative growth of teachers in secondary schools in Period-1 became less negative in Period-2. The C.V. value was relatively smaller in Period-2 than in Period-1. The results reveal the need to employ more teachers in the years to come, if the spread on education had to be sustained in its present expansion stage in India.

Enrolment of students is a measure of immediate attainment in education. The enrolment of males and females at different levels of education is presented in Table 2.6. The enrolment of students in primary, secondary and high/higher secondary schools was 76.16 million, 21.94 million and 12.55 million respectively in 1981-82. It increased to 97.4 million, 34 million and 19.1 million in 1990-91 and 122.31 million, 47.26 million and 34 million in 2004-05. It shows that there is a steady increase in the total enrolment in the schools. The mean values were significantly larger with relatively lesser C.V. value in Period-2. It was relatively larger for primary schools in Period-2. But the growth rate was less for the enrolment in primary and secondary schools in Period-2. It was higher for high/higher secondary schools in Period-2. Thus, the enrolment in schools shows an uptrend with larger mean values and smaller C.V. and CGR value during the post-reform period.

The analysis of enrolment of male and female students in primary, secondary and higher secondary shown has similar results as seen in the total enrolment of students. Thus, the enrolment in schools shows a significant increase with larger mean and relatively lesser C.V. and CGR for Period-2 as compared to Period-1, the inference being that during the post-economic reform period the enrolment significantly increased in schools, especially in high/higher secondary schools.

The literacy rate is an important indicator of educational attainment. The details are presented in Table 2.7. The total literacy rate increased in Period-1 by 6.02 per cent and in Period-2 by 16.78 per cent. The male and female literacy rates also increased by 9.34 per cent and 4.51 per cent in Period-1 and

Table 2.6
Enrolment by Levels of Education

(in millions)

Years	*Primary*			*Secondary*			*High/Higher*		
	M	*F*	*T*	*M*	*F*	*T*	*M*	*F*	*T*
(1)	*(2)*	*(3)*	*(4)*	*(5)*	*(6)*	*(7)*	*(8)*	*(9)*	*(10)*
Period-1									
1981-82	46.77	29.39	76.16	14.67	7.28	21.94	8.93	3.61	12.55
1982-83	48.66	30.87	79.53	15.63	7.51	23.13	9.81	3.94	13.75
1983-84	50.31	32.24	82.55	16.59	8.59	25.17	10.22	4.26	14.48
1984-85	51.96	33.72	85.68	17.14	9.03	26.17	10.84	4.63	15.47
1985-86	52.20	35.20	87.40	17.70	9.60	27.30	11.50	5.00	16.50
1986-87	51.73	35.43	87.16	17.80	9.65	27.45	11.47	5.17	16.65
1987-88	53.62	36.91	90.53	18.81	10.43	29.25	10.87	4.95	15.82
1988-89	53.85	37.36	91.22	19.22	10.71	29.93	10.98	5.27	16.25
1989-90	54.33	38.05	92.37	19.77	11.10	30.88	11.72	5.64	17.36
1990-91	57.00	40.40	97.40	21.50	12.50	34.00	12.80	6.30	19.10
Mean	52.04	34.96	87.00	17.88	09.64	27.52	10.91	04.88	15.79

(Contd.)

TABLE 2.6 (Contd.)

(1)	(2)	(3)	(4)	(5)	(6)	(7)	(8)	(9)	(10)
C.V	05.65	09.80	07.29	11.33	16.82	13.26	09.90	16.45	11.82
C.G.R	01.82*	03.29*	02.41*	03.77*	05.70*	04.44*	02.98*	05.49*	03.74*
				Period-2					
1991-92	58.60	42.30	100.9	22.00	13.60	35.60	13.50	06.90	20.40
1992-93	57.90	41.70	99.60	21.20	12.90	34.10	13.60	06.90	20.50
1993-94	55.10	41.90	97.00	20.60	13.50	34.10	13.20	07.50	20.70
1994-95	60.00	45.10	105.10	22.10	14.30	36.40	14.20	07.90	22.10
1995-96	60.90	46.20	107.10	22.70	14.80	37.50	14.60	08.30	22.90
1996-97	61.40	46.80	108.20	22.90	15.20	38.10	16.30	08.70	25.00
1997-98	62.30	48.00	110.30	23.60	15.90	39.50	16.10	09.30	25.40
1998-99	62.70	48.20	110.90	24.00	16.30	40.30	17.30	10.50	27.80
1999-00	64.10	49.50	113.60	25.10	17.00	42.10	17.20	11.00	28.20
2000-01	64.00	49.80	113.80	25.30	17.50	42.80	16.90	10.70	27.60
2001-02	65.12	50.23	115.35	25.85	17.84	43.69	17.26	11.02	28.28
2002-03	66.45	51.42	117.87	26.12	18.25	44.37	18.56	11.85	30.41
2003-04	67.85	52.32	120.17	27.56	18.63	46.19	19.85	12.05	31.90
2004-05	69.42	52.89	122.31	28.14	19.12	47.26	20.74	13.26	34.00

Mean	62.56	47.60	110.16	24.08	16.06	40.14	16.38	9.71	26.09
C.V	06.35	07.93	06.98	09.68	12.81	10.88	14.42	21.15	16.81
C.G.R	01.46*	01.90*	01.65*	02.26*	03.11*	02.59*	03.38*	05.22*	04.05*
t(m)f	-07.08*	-08.20*	-07.80*	-06.77*	-08.20*	-07.40*	-06,80*	-07.05*	-06.95*

Note : C.G.R — Compound growth rate.
C.V — Coefficient of variation,
* Significant at one per cent level.
t (m) — 't' test values for difference between means of two periods.

15.94 per cent and 17.98 per cent in Period-2. It indicates that the increase in literacy was less for females than for males in Period-1, but it was reversed largely in Period-2. Thus, the post-economic reform period witnessed increase in literacy rate especially for females.

EDUCATIONAL ATTAINMENT AND ECONOMIC DEVELOPMENT

Given the other resources, the economic development of a country mostly depends on the development of human resources through education, training and health. Therefore, the relationship between educational attainment and economic development was studied for their strength and the direction of causality. That is, the impact of educational attainment (proxied by the proportion of the population allocated to higher education institutions, i.e., number of students enrolled per capita in general education, engineering education, and medical education) of the level on growth rate of GDP per capita at constant (1993-94) prices was studied.

In order to test causality between education attainment and economic development, two different sets of variables for education were used. First, the causality link between the number of students per institution enrolled in higher education (education attainment in general education—GEN, engineering education—ENG, and medical education—MED) and GDP per capita at (1993-94) constant prices. The focus here is on the relationship between the intensity of the efforts made by a society concerning educational attainment and their level on economic development. Secondly, the link between the rates of growth of these variables (GRGEN, GRENG, and GRMED) and GDP per capita was attempted.

The focus here is to examine the causality between increase in education attainment and economic growth. The data used for this purpose was for a period of 24 years, from 1981-82 to 2004-05. The Augmented Dickey Fuller (ADF) test was carried out for the actual data and growth rates (in percentage values). The results show that both actual data and growth rates are stationary. Hence, the test for causality between educational attainment and economic development was carried out directly

TABLE 2.7
Male and Female Literacy Rates (%)

Years	*M*	*F*	*T*	*F/M Ratio*
		Period-1		
1981-82	54.50	29.75	43.56	54.59
1982-83	55.63	30.25	43.85	54.38
1983-84	56.35	30.65	44.10	54.39
1984-85	56.93	21.41	44.75	37.61
1985-86	58.08	31.65	45.02	54.49
1986-87	59.24	31.90	45.94	53.85
1987-88	60.39	32.34	46.85	53.55
1988-89	61.54	32.98	47.76	53.59
1989-90	62.69	33.62	48.67	53.63
1990-91	63.84	34.26	49.58	53.67
		Period-2		
1991-92	68.00	39.00	52.00	60.94
1992-93	68.00	43.00	56.00	63.24
1993-94	69.00	44.00	57.00	63.77
1994-95	69.00	46.00	58.00	66.67
1995-96	70.00	47.00	59.00	67.14
1996-97	71.60	50.00	60.85	69.83
1997-98	72.50	52.30	61.25	72.14
1998-99	73.45	53.45	62.45	72.77
1999-00	74.15	53.94	63.65	72.74
2000-01	75.85	54.16	65.38	71.40
2001-02	77.67	55.25	66.12	71.13
2002-03	78.52	55.96	66.95	71.27
2003-04	79.75	56.25	67.56	70.53
2004-05	79.94	56.98	68.78	71.28

within the classical framework of Granger (1969) for actual data and growth rates.

The results obtained from the Granger's Causality Test are given in Table 2.8. The results also confirm the presents of causality link between education attainment and economic

TABLE 2.8
Results of Bi-Variate Granger's Causality Test

Equations	*Dependent Variable*	*Causal Variable*	*'F' Statistic for Causality Test*
(1)	GDP	GED	F(2,15) = 57.26*
	GED	GDP	F(2,15) = 4.15@
(2)	GDP	EED	F(2,15) = 38.11*
	EED	GDP	F(2,15) = 9.48*
(3)	GDP	MED	F(2,15) = 61.33*
	MED	GDP	F(2,15) = 34.77*
(4)	GRGDP	GRGED	F(1,17) = 12.04*
	GRGED	GRGDP	F(1,17) = 4.32@
(5)	GRGDP	GREED	F(1,17) = 83.69*
	GREED	GRGDP	F(1,17) = 54.58*
(6)	GRGDP	GRMED	F(1,17) = 11.21*
	GRMED	GRGDP	F(1,17) = 33.72*

Note : Lag length for the variables of actual data and growth rate (GR) were two and one respectively for independent variables.
* Significant at one per cent level.
@ Not significant at five per cent level.

development. The causality link was one directional between GED and GDP both in actual data and growth rates. It means that economic development contributed for general education but the reverse was not so. There was bi-directional causal relationship between engineering education and economic development and medical education and economic development, both in actual data and growth rates. It confirmed the presence of causality link from engineering and medical education to economic development, and from economic development to engineering and medical education. It suggested the presence of a long-run stable linear relationship between education attainment and economic development. Even for GED to GDP, there was a long-run linear relationship but that relationship was not significant as found in actual data and growth rates.

The results of causality analysis suggested that education attainment increased the labour productivity and thereby contributed to economic development, even though the link between education attainment and economic development was complex. Intuitively, one would come to the conclusion from empirical results that, education attainment through expansion of general education, engineering education and medical education, and educational attainment contributed to economic growth during the period of the study.

SUMMARY OF FINDINGS

The following are the findings of the study:

- The expenditure on education reveals a steady increase but at lower rate during the post-economic reform period. There was structural change between two periods in the different components of educational expenditure.
- The elasticity for the different components of educational expenditure with respect to GDP declined for all governments in period-2.
- Though the number of primary schools and secondary schools per lakh population increased, but the primary schools have not increased consistently with the increase in size of population.
- The number of teachers per 10,000 students shows a steady increase in primary schools but at lesser rate in secondary schools. It is because the governments have accorded priority to increase the number of teachers in primary schools with the goal of enrolling all eligible students at that level.
- The enrolment of males and females in primary, secondary and high/higher secondary schools shows an uptrend, especially in high/higher secondary schools during post-economic reform period.
- The male and female literacy has increased in both the periods but at a higher rate in period-2, showing that the new economic reform policy increased the literacy

rate, especially for females during post-economic reform period.

- The Granger's Causality Test proved that there is a stable and precise relationship between educational attainment and economic development in India during the period of the study, via, 1981-82 to 2004-05. This might be attributed to increase in labour productivity by educational attainments.

This study analyses the growth of educational expenditure of the governments. It has been analysed for its impact on infrastructural development and attainment and thereby economic development ultimately. There is bi-directional causality between educational development and consequently on economic development. The comparative study of pre- and post-reform periods shows that the NERP has a positive impact on educational development, which in turn on economic development. The results show that educational development and economic development are complementary to each other.

As educational development and economic development are interacting and impacting on each other, economic growth is a necessary condition for educational development and gender parity in development. The emphasis on attaining eight per cent to ten per cent annual growth in real GDP (economic growth) is a right policy and efforts to achieve the target have to be intensified.

References

Barrera, Albina (1990) "The Role of Maternal Schooling and Its Interaction with Public Health Programs in child Health Production", *Journal of Development Economics*, 32(1).

Bhatty, Kiran (1998) "Educational Deprivation in India—A Survey of Field Investigations", *Economic and Political Weekly*, 23(28).

Chaubey, P.K. and Chaubey, Geeta (1998) "Gender Equity Sensitive Literacy Rates: An Alternative Approach", *Anvesak*, 28(1).

Ghosh, Arun. (1992) "Education for All—The Financing Problem", *Economic and Political Weekly*, April 4.

Gosal (1964) "Inequalities in the Levels of Literacy: A Regional Analysis", *Occasional Paper* (4), New Delhi, NIEPA.

Haldar, Sisir Kumar (1969) "Public Expenditure on Education—The Search for Criteria," *Yojana*, July 27.

Karlekar, Malavika (2000) "Girl's Access to Schooling: An Assessment", in Rakha Wazir (ed), *The Gender Gap in Basic Education,* New Delhi, Sage Publications.

M.A., Hussain (1981) "Continuing Education and Its Role in Human Resource Development in India", *Journal of Higher Education,* 7(1).

Mehrotra, Santosh (2006) *The Economics of Elementary Education in India: The Challenge of Public Provisioning and Household Costs,* New Delhi, Sage Publication.

Nambissan, Seetha B. (1996) "Equity in Education? Schooling of Dalit Children in India", *Economic and Political Weekly,* 31(16&17).

Pulparampil, John (1999) "Educational HRD", *New Frontier in Education,* 24(4).

3

Role of Education in Economic Development— An Interstate Analysis

ALKA SAMRA

The Indian economy has experienced an average annual growth rate of around 6 per cent during the last two decades. When it is compared to several East Asian economies, this is quite impressive. In terms of per capita income, the improvement has been around 4 per cent per annum in the recent period as compared to less than 1.5 per cent in the earlier period. Further, there has been a steady acceleration in the growth performance over the years. But the problem of regional disparity within the country is increasingly becoming a matter of great concern for policy-makers. In a vast and varied country like India this is a natural phenomenon. The Indian economy presents a very deplorable picture of inter-regional disparities reflected in income distribution, urbanization, agriculture, education, industrial production and the position of infrastructure in different states. There are many economic, historical, geographical and political causes behind regional disparities. The important cause of growing disparities is the difference in natural and created endowments in different states. As per the poor performance in irrigation and power sectors, the green revolution in Bihar and Rajasthan has not turned as green as in the Punjab, Haryana, Tamil Nadu and Uttar Pradesh.

The causes of disparities are the unequal distribution of public revenue among the states. During all the years of planning considerable investment has been concentrated at a few places like Mumbai, Ahmedabad, Delhi, Kanpur, Kolkata, Chennai and Bangalore etc. And the flow of capital and concentration of economic power continue to be biased in favour of large cities and the location of functions and facilities continues to be urban biased due to market imperfections such as factor immobility, price rigidity, ignorance of market conditions, lack of specializations and lack of division of labour, etc.

Education is a critical input for investment in human capital. As against the goal of 6 per cent of GDP, the total expenditure on education in India is currently 3.99 per cent of GDP (2001-02). Plan expenditure on education has also increased rapidly since the First Five Year Plan. A high priority has been accorded to this sector in the Tenth Five Year Plan, with an allocation of Rs. 43,825 crore as against Rs. 24,908 crore made in the Ninth Plan, representing an increase of 76 per cent. During the Tenth Plan Rs. 28,750 crore has been allocated for elementary education. It shows that education in every sense is one of the fundamental factors of development. No country can achieve sustainable economic development without substantial investment in human capital. In spite of this growth in education expenditure, great disparity in education is found in India. The present study, therefore, attempts to show educational disparities in India and its impact on economic development.

OBJECTIVES OF THE STUDY

The main objectives of the study are:

1. To identify regional disparities in education and economic development.
2. To examine the inter-relationship between education and economic development.

METHODOLOGY

To derive a composite index from a set of variables, a wide variety of multivariate statistical techniques are available. One needs to look for an alternative dimension reduction technique which will summarize the whole set of information into a manageable form without much loss of the information related to original data. Though the composite index can be built up using simple techniques like ranking and indexing methods, but these techniques have many drawbacks which have been criticized by the Dandekar Committee (1984), Kundu and Raza (1982) and Sarker (1995). The main drawbacks are arbitrariness and allocation of equal weights.

In this study the Principal Component Analysis is used. A set of original variables is transformed to a new set of uncorrelated variables called principal components. These new variables are linear functions of the original variables and derived in decreasing order of importance. The objective is to find out only a few components which account for most of the variations in the original data set. It reduced a set of variables to much smaller size without losing the properties of the data.

The Education Development Index is a composite of these variables:

1. Adult literacy rate.
2. Enrollment rate (Percentage of enrollment in 6-14 age group).
3. Number of primary schools per thousand population.
4. Percentage of habitations having educational amenities.
5. Teacher-pupil ratio.

In order to assess the role of education in economic development, the Composite Index of Economic Development is also computed with the help of these variables:

1. Per Capita Gross Domestic Product at Constant Price (1993-94=100).
2. Per Capita Consumption Expenditure for 30 Days.
3. Percentage of People above Poverty Line.
4. Employment Rate.

After computing the composite index of economic development, it is correlated with education development using Karl Pearson's Correlation of Coefficient.

EMPIRICAL ANALYSIS

Five variables have been considered for education development index. The loading structure and other related statistics are depicted in the Table 3.1.

TABLE 3.1
Principal Component Loading and Coefficient of Variation for Educational Variables

Sl. No.	*Variables*	*Mean*	*Factor Loading*	*Coefficient of variation*
1.	Adult literacy rate	63.88	.42807	17.78%
2.	Percentage of enrollment in 6-14 age group	94.25	.70845	15.68%
3.	Primary schools per thousand population	1.179	.70636	51.06%
4.	Percentage of habitations having educational amenities	79.39	-.37845	17.94%
5.	Teacher-pupil ratio	34.42	-.73938	37.19%
	Variation explained		37.4%	

Source : Computed.

It is observed from Table 3.1 that percentage of enrollment in 6-14 age group has the highest (.70845) loading in the principal component and it explains the maximum correlation followed by primary schools per thousand population and adult literacy rate. It is also found from Table 3.1 that percentage of habitations having educational amenities and teacher-pupil ratio does not play significant role in educational development. Table 3.1 depicts that the average adult literacy rate is only 63.88 per cent. It affects the enrollment ratio and seems that almost 6 per cent children are not enrolled in the schools. It is surprising to say that the average number of primary schools per thousand is only 1.179.

The regional disparity in educational development has also been examined by coefficient of variation as shown in Table 3.1. It is seen that highest variation (51.06 per cent) is found in primary schools per thousand population followed by teacher-pupil ratio (37.19 per cent) and percentage of habitations having educational amenities (17.94 per cent).

Four variables for economic development have been considered for the construction of economic development index. The loading structure and other related statistics are depicted in Table 3.2.

TABLE 3.2

Principal Component Loading and Coefficient of Variation for Educational Variables

Sl. No.	*Variables*	*Mean*	*Factor Loading*	*Coefficient of variation (in per cent)*
1.	Per capita Gross Domestic Product (Rs.)	11916.28	.83747	36.68
2.	Per capita consumption expenditure (Rs.)	622.98	.96262	21.09
3.	Percentage of people above poverty line (%)	77.12	.87767	15.28
4.	Employment rate (%)	80.37	-.12082	18.33
	Variation explained		60.3%	

Source : Computed.

It is observed from Table 3.2 that per capita consumption expenditure has the highest loading (.96262) in the principal component followed by percentage of people above poverty line and per capita gross domestic product. The employment rate is not as significant as compared to other factors for economic development. Table 3.2 also shows that on an average one Indian national consumes only Rs. 622.98 worth of things that are absolutely necessary in a month. Low per capita income leads to lower consumption expenditure. Only 77.12 per cent of India's population lives above the poverty line. In other words, 22.88 per cent of the total population still lives below the poverty line and 19.63 per cent population is unemployed. Thus, the basic problem of India lies in the circle of poverty, hunger and economic imbalance.

The regional disparity in economic development has also been examined by coefficient of variation shown in Table 3.2. It as shows that highest variation (36.68 per cent) is found in per capita gross domestic product followed by per capita consumption expenditure (21.09 per cent) and employment rate (18.33 per cent).

COMPOSITE INDEX OF EDUCATION AND ECONOMIC DEVELOPMENT

By using the above mentioned factor loadings education development index and economic development index are computed and presented in Table 3.3. It depicts that the highest value of the state indicates top position for both education and economic development. The value of the education development index varies from -0.56 to 2.25. Himachal Pradesh is on the top position with 2.25 value followed by Jammu and Kashmir (1-33) and Madhya Pradesh with the value 1.25. On the other side Bihar (-0.56) has the lowest value followed by Uttar Pradesh (0.07) and West Bengal (0.15).

Table 3.3 also shows the index value of economic development. The value of economic development varies from 3.37 to 1.51. Punjab is on the top with a value of 3.37 followed by Haryana (3.25) and Gujarat (3.10). Bihar is the poorest (1.51) of all followed by Orissa (1.61) and Madhya Pradesh (1.89).

TABLE 3.3
Education Development Index and Economic Development Index (2004-05)

Sl. No.	*States*	*Education Development Index*		*Economic Development Index*	
		Value	*Rank*	*Value*	*Rank*
1.	Andhra Pradesh	0.78	8	2.54	10
2.	Assam	1.24	4	2.07	13
3.	Bihar	-0.56	17	1.51	17
4.	Gujarat	0.45	12	3.10	3
5.	Haryana	0.26	14	3.25	2
6.	Himachal Pradesh	2.25	1	3.03	5
7.	Jammu & Kashmir	1.33	2	2.75	8
8.	Karnataka	0.69	10	2.67	9
9.	Kerala	0.55	11	3.07	4
10.	Madhya Pradesh	1.25	3	1.89	15
11.	Maharashtra	0.75	9	3.02	6
12.	Orissa	0.94	6	1.61	16
13.	Punjab	0.36	13	3.37	1
14.	Rajasthan	0.97	5	2.35	12
15.	Tamil Nadu	0.83	7	2.84	7
16.	Uttar Pradesh	0.07	16	1.90	14
17.	West Bengal	0.15	15	2.49	11

Source : Computed.

CLUSTER ANALYSIS ACCORDING TO EDUCATION DEVELOPMENT INDEX

According to the Education Development Index, the states are classified into three groups, i.e. high, moderate and low developed regions. The state-wise classification is shown in Table 3.4.

Table 3.4 shows a clear-cut dominance of moderately developed region (58.83 per cent) followed by low (29.41 per cent) and high developed region (11.76 per cent) respectively.

TABLE 3.4
Clustering of States According to Education Development Index

Group	*Value*	*State*		
		No.	*%*	*Name*
High developed	2.25-1.31	2	11.76	Himachal Pradesh, Jammu & Kashmir
Moderately developed	1.31-0.37	10	58.83	Andhra Pradesh, Assam, Gujarat, Karnataka, Kerala, Madhya Pradesh, Orissa, Rajasthan, Tamil Nadu
Low developed	0.37-(-0.57)	5	29.41	Bihar, Haryana, Punjab, Uttar Pradesh, West Bengal
Total		17	100	

Source : Computed.

The value of high developed regions ranges between 3.37 and 2.75. It consists of only two states, i.e. Himachal Pradesh and Jammu & Kashmir. Bihar, Haryana, Punjab, Uttar Pradesh and West Bengal show the low level of educational development due to less enrollment ratio and adult literacy rate.

CLUSTER ANALYSIS ACCORDING TO ECONOMIC DEVELOPMENT INDEX

According to the Economic Development Index, the states are classified into three clusters, i.e. high, moderately and low developed regions. State-wise classification is shown in Table 3.5.

Table 3.5 shows the clear-cut dominance of high developed regions (47.06 per cent) followed by low (29.41 per cent) and moderately developed regions (23.53 per cent). Assam, Bihar, Madhya Pradesh, Orissa and Uttar Pradesh comprises the low developed region because the per capita gross domestic product of these states is low and the percentage of people above poverty line is also very less compared to other states.

TABLE 3.5
Clustering of States According to Economic Development Index

Group	*Value*	*State*		
		No.	*%*	*Name*
High developed	3.37 - 2.75	8	47.06	Gujarat, Haryana, Himachal Pradesh, Jammu & Kashmir, Kerala, Maharashtra, Punjab, Tamil Nadu
Moderately developed	2.75 - 2.13	4	23.53	Andhra Pradesh, Karnataka, Rajasthan, West Bengal
Low developed	2.13 - .51	5	29.41	Assam, Bihar, Madhya Pradesh, Orissa, Uttar Pradesh
Total		17	100	

Source : Computed.

RELATIONSHIP BETWEEN EDUCATION AND ECONOMIC DEVELOPMENT

Education enriches people's understanding of themselves and the world. It improves the quality of their lives and leads to broad social benefits to individuals and society. Education raises people's productivity and creativity and promotes entrepreneurship and technological advances. It plays a crucial role in securing economic and social progress and improving income distribution. Education brings all the positive changes in variable factors of production as well as in infrastructure development. It can be said that education is a pillar on which the major part of an economy stands. If the pillar is strong enough to hold the economy, the irregularities can be reduced very easily and the economy will multiply. And if the pillar of education is weak and fragile, the irregularities may push the economy downward and the economy may fall down. Thus, economic development depends on the qualitative workforce and this qualitative workforce can be acquired by developing professional, social and communication skills through education.

To examine the relationship between education and economic development, Karl Pearson's correlation coefficient is computed. The correlation coefficient is:

Correlation Coefficient Between Education Development Index and Economic Development Index r = 0.167

The result indicates that the relationship between education and economic development is significant at 5 per cent level of significance. Although the 'r' value (0.167) is very low but education is positively correlated with economic development. It shows that education is indispensable to economic development. No economic development is possible without good education. A balanced education system promotes not only economic development, but productivity and income per capita. Its influence is noticeable at the micro-level of an individual family. Although the correlation is positive but it is low. It explains that education is not the only one sector which influences economic development but the other sectors, i.e. agriculture, infrastructure, industrial development are also responsible for development.

The state-wise comparison of education and economic development is presented in Table 3.6. It is seen that high educational development of states gives rise to high economic development. There are only two states: Himachal Pradesh and Jammu & Kashmir which comprises high educational development and economic development. On the other side Bihar and Uttar Pradesh comprises low education and low economic development. It is seen from Table 3.6 that although Gujarat, Kerala, Maharashtra and Tamil Nadu are economically developed states but their educational development is still moderate.

It is surprising to see that although the education development of Haryana and Punjab is low but their economic development is high because the economy of these two states is agriculture-based and the share of agriculture is high in gross domestic product. The share of Haryana and Punjab is 29.3 per

TABLE 3.6
State-wise Comparison of Education and Economic Development

Education development		Economic development		
	Level	*High*	*Moderate*	*Low*
	High	Himachal Pradesh, Jammu & Kashmir	—	—
	Moderate	Gujarat, Kerala, Maharashtra, Tamil Nadu	Andhra Pradesh, Karnataka, Rajasthan	Assam, Madhya Pradesh, Orissa
	Low	Haryana, Punjab	West Bengal	Bihar, Uttar Pradesh

Source : Computed.

cent and 38.6 percent respectively. Further the share of agriculture in total employment of Haryana and Punjab is 50.3 per cent and 45.6 per cent respectively. It seems that although Punjab and Haryana are educationally backward, but they proved economically forward due to agriculture-based economy. Thus, economic development not only depends on education but the other sectors are also equally important for economic development.

CONCLUSION

In general, development can be viewed as a multi-dimensional phenomenon. It means the improvement of people's life styles through improved education, income, skill development and employment. Here, a composite index of education and economic development is constructed. The findings of the analysis support the general perception about the states. The states in India are marked with wide disparity in education and economic development. Some states are better in terms of economic development while states like Kerala and Tamil Nadu have recorded remarkable social progress. The role of education in promoting basic capabilities emerges as the prerequisite to economic development. Faster development requires government action to improve elementary education.

Kerala has set-up the example and has clearly established the primary benchmark for other states in India. Although expanding gross domestic product and other related variables is one of the most fundamental input to economic development, but the basic objective of development should focus on the expansion of human capabilities, i.e. education which has been neglected for long in India.

References

Agarwal, A.N. (1991) *Indian Economy: Problems of Development and Planning,* New Delhi, Wiley Eastern Limited.

Dandekar, V.M. (1995) *The Indian Economy, 1947-92, Population, Poverty and Employment,* Vol. 2, New Delhi, Sage Publications.

Das, A. (2001) *Socio-Economic Development in India, Development and Society.*

Government of India, (2004) *Statistical Abstract of India.*

Hall, P. (1983) *Growth and Development,* Oxford.

Kundu, A. and Raja, M. (1982) *Indian Economy: The Regional Dimension,* New Delhi, Spectrum Publishers.

Sarker, P.C. (1998) *Regional Disparities in India: Issues and Measurement,* Bombay, Himalaya Publishing House.

Sen, A. (1997) *Indian Development: Selected Regional Perspective.*

4

Education, Growth and Wages in India—An Inter-relationship

KULDEEP KAUR

INTRODUCTION

Investment in people plays a key role and appears attractive relative to investment in alternative assets. It is seen both as an essential growth factor and key level of social cohesion policy. There is a broad consensus in the academic literature that human capital is a determinant of productivity and other economic outcomes, both at the individual and at the aggregate level. Its role is particularly crucial in today's knowledge-driven economy which plays a key role in fostering technological change and diffusion of technology. Human capital is a broad and multifaceted concept encompassing different types of investment in people. Health and education are certainly important aspects of such investment, particularly in the developing countries like India. Here, deficiency in these respects may severely limit the population's ability to engage in productive activities.This is because human capital represents skills, knowledge, ability to labour and good health that together enable people to pursue different livelihood strategies to achieve their livelihood objectives. The practical knowledge acquired skills and learned abilities of an individual that make him or her to earn income in exchange for labour, is commonly termed as human capital. The key aspect of human capital is related to the knowledge and skills embodied in people that are accumulated through schooling, training and experience. They are useful in the production of goods, services and further knowledge.

Available evidence suggests that the importance of education as input has grown over time as production processes have become increasingly knowledge intensive. Workers with greater problem-solving and communication abilities are likely to perform better than their less skilled counterparts. Hence, skilled workers can be expected to be more productive than unskilled ones for any given production and are expected to operate more sophisticated technologies that place greater demand on their capacities.

The hypothesis that human capital is a key determinant of productivity has received considerable attention. At micro-level labour economists have long been concerned with labour market outcomes. However, building in this work, macro-economists have been using growth accounting techniques to analyze the contribution of education to aggregate economic growth since the 1960s. Research in the second area has received a new impulse in recent years with the development of a new generation of theoretical models that attribute to the accumulation of knowledge and skills. The construction of cross–country data sets can be used in empirical analysis of determinants of economic growth.

While traditional neo-classical models focused almost exclusively on the accumulation of physical capital, more recent contributions have attributed increased importance to the accumulation of human capital and productive knowledge and the interaction between the two. The 'new growth theory' emphasizes the importance of education in the creation of new knowledge and in the growth of living standards over time (Riddell, 2001). The need for appropriate human capital development and accumulation is a prerequisite for modern economic growth in both developed and developing economies.

The relevance of human capital accumulation in the process of economic development stems from its potential beneficial impact on macro-economic productivity and on the long run distribution of incomes, once some basic conditions are met. The 1960s and early 1970s were marked in the Western world mostly by an enthusiasm for the issue of education and its presumed positive impact on economic growth. Schultz advocates treating education as an investment in men and its consequences as a form of capital. This enthusiasm for education led to various attempts at measuring both capital and the rate of returns on investment in education such that the expenditure on education becomes an investment rather than consumption. To measure costs and benefits of education, Schultz (1960) formulated the following hypothesis: "Some important increase, in national income are a consequence of additions to the stock of this form of capital". The formulation of this 'kind of capital' is probably responsible for the 'unexplained' increases in the national income. After this the issue of education and its impact on the long-term economic growth started to dominate social science discourse. The line of thinking, for example, was explored by Denison (1967). The dominant hypothesis was that education affects positively the economic growth since it increases the level of cognitive skills possessed by the labour force and consequently its marginal productivity. Eventually, the debate among the economists shifted during the 1980s to the impact of technology combined with knowledge and skills on economic growth. This was partly as a response to the criticism voiced by the development economists. It became obvious that technical change could not be seen independently from human interaction, and therefore from human capital. Technology could not be seen separately from the human inputs that create them to utilize them. Easterlin (1981) using a historical approach has pointed out that limited diffusion of technology is the cause of slow growth in the developing countries. According to him this limitation, in turn, is linked to both the quantity and quality of educational system. In other empirical studies, increasing attention has been paid to the role of education in explaining a country's economic growth. According to Wang and Yao (2003) using national data from 1978 to 1999 human capital stock, measured by average years of schooling, contributed 11 per cent of GDP growth in the reform period. Based on provincial data from 1978 to 1989, using higher education enrollment as an indicator of human capital accumulation, Chen and Feng (2000) found that education has a positive and significant effect on economic growth. Chen and Fleisher (1996) found a statistically insignificant relationship between human capital investment and growth at the provincial level when their measure of human capital was in terms of secondary schooling. However, in a later study Fleisher and Chen (1997) found a positive relationship between human capital and growth in total factor productivity.

This way, the conventional wisdom on the role of education in economic growth is being revised in terms of both theory and new evidence. Tertiary education or higher education is now considered critical from the standpoint of achieving overall economic and social development. Thus, rising premium on higher education reflects the growing demand for skills driven in large part by the spread of new technologies. Recent research suggests that increase in the number of skilled workers may have boosted the value of further education and made it more important for growth. Indeed in many countries building a work force with higher order skills is an important part of improving the climate for investment, acquiring a competitive edge and generally maintaining an engine of growth (*World Development Report*, 2007).

Lee (2006) in his paper has tried to shed light on the educational attainment as a factor effecting the speed of transition movement of labour force from agricultural sector to non-agricultural sector. Barro (1998) has analyzed the determinants of economic growth and investment in about one hundred countries over the period from 1960 to 1995. With respect to education he found that growth is positively related to the average years of schooling attainment of adult males at the secondary and higher levels. Growth is insignificantly related to school attainment of females because women are not well utilized in the labour market. Abril (2003) highlights that women have almost reached the same level of education as men in some countries, while in others they have surpassed men. Despite this women continue to participate less in the labour market and earn less than men.

The following major conclusions can be drawn from the various studies that have been undertaken on education and growth relationship. (i) Educational attainment indicators are highly correlated with the wealth level of countries, in particular, mass primary education has positive impact on growth, (ii) Different levels of education have different impacts on growth depending upon the stage of economic development reached by various countries and also on the quality of education (iii) Higher education boosts economic growth in a greater way (iv) Economic returns to investment in education for women are significantly lower than men because of low participation rates of women in the labour market, (v) Returns to education in urban areas are likely to be higher than rural areas because of poor school quality, and (vi) Educated workers are likely to reap more benefits than uneducated because of better employment prospects. It is in this context that the present study aims at studying the impact of different levels of education on the economic growth of various states of India with the following specific objectives:

1. To study the relationship between Net State Domestic Products (NSDP) of major states of India and levels of education in three major sectors (primary, secondary and tertiary) of these states.
2. To study the impact of education levels on the wages in major industry groups over a period of time (i.e. for 1990-2000).
3. To analyze the relationship between male and female education at various levels of education and per capita.
4. To study the relationship between rural and urban education at various levels and per capita NSDP.
5. To draw some policy implications and conclusions from the study.

The study is divided into three main sections including the present one. The second part discusses database and methodology. The third one highlights major findings of the study and draws some conclusions and policy implications.

II

DATABASE AND METHODOLOGY

This Section proposes to study the relationship between share of the three sectors (primary, secondary and tertiary) in Net State Domestic Product and levels of education, i.e. illiterate, primary, middle and secondary and above (as an indicator of human capital). This was to study the relationship between economic growth and human capital formation in 17 major states of India and at the all India level for the year 1999-2000. Secondary or higher secondary level of schooling and other higher qualifications have been taken as the dividing line between educated and uneducated workers. For analytical convenience those with primary and/or middle level schooling are categorized as semi-educated workers. Going by this classification, illiterate workers are synonymous with low-quality workers, semi-educated workers represent medium quality workers, and educated workers, as defined above are proxies for high quality workers (Chadha, 2004). However, the main source of data regarding different education levels of workers in the major states and major industry groups is the household level data on CD-ROM for the year 1999-2000 supplied by NSSO, New Delhi. Data regarding the wages of the workers for the year 1999-2000 have been collected from various reports of the Centre for Monitoring Indian Economy (CMIE). The CSO compiled data on NSDP has been used to get sectoral composition of NSDP for 17 major states of India for the year 1999-2000 at constant prices (1993-94=00).

Data for 26 major states of India for net attendance ratios total enrolment as per cent of their total population for rural and urban males, rural and urban females for different education levels have been compiled from manpower profile. Four to five years of lagged regression equations have been fitted to analyze the impact of education on per capita net state domestic product, as children enrolled in a particular year will not enter the labour force immediately, but after completing certain years of schooling.

To compute the impact of education on economic growth simple regression analysis has been used. These equations are of the form.

Agriculture Sector

1. $NSDP_{AS} = f(PPW)$
2. $NSDP_{AS} = f(PMW)$
3. $NSDP_{AS} = f(PSW)$

Secondary Sector

1. $NSDP_{SS} = f(PPW)$
2. $NSDP_{SS} = f(PMW)$
3. $NSDP_{SS} = f(PSW)$

Tertiary Sector

1. $NSDP_{TS} = f(PPW)$
2. $NSDP_{TS} = f(PMW)$
3. $NSDP_{TS} = f(PSW)$

$NSDP_{AS}$ = Per cent Share of Respective State's Agricultural Sector in its Net State Domestic Product in 1999-2000.

$NSDP_{SS}$ = Per cent Share of Respective State's Secondary Sector in its Net State Domestic Product in 1999-2000.

$NSDP_{TS}$ = Per cent Share of Respective State's Tertiary Sector in its Net State Domestic Product in 1999-2000.

PPW = Per cent of workers (Principal Status) having Primary Level of Education.

PMW = Per cent of workers (Principal Status) having Middle Level of Education.

PSW = Per cent of workers (Principal Status) having Secondary and above level of Education.

To explain the impact of human capital formation on wages of the workers in major industry

1. $W_{99-00} = f(PPW_{99-00})$
2. $W_{99-00} = f(PMW_{99-00})$
3. $W_{99-00} = f(PSW_{99-00})$

where

W_{99-00} = Wages of the workers in respective industry group in the year 1999-2000.

PPW_{99-00} = Percentage of the workers in the respective industry group having primary level of education 1999-00.

PMW_{99-00} = Percentage of the workers in the respective industry group having middle level of education 1999-00.

PSW_{99-00} = Percentage of the workers in the respective industry group having secondary and above level of education 1999-00.

To analyze the impact of net attendance ratio of males, females in rural and urban areas, on per capita net state domestic product following legged equations have been fitted:

1. $PC\ NSDP_{99-00} = f(UM\ NAR_{95-96})$
2. $PC\ NSDP_{99-00} = f(UF\ NAR_{95-96})$
3. $PC\ NSDP_{99-00} = f(RM\ NAR_{95-96})$
4. $PC\ NSDP_{99-00} = f(RF\ NAR_{95-96})$
5. $PC\ NSDP_{2004-05} = f(TMER_{2000-01})$
6. $PC\ NSDP_{2004-05} = f(TFER_{2000-01})$

where :

1. PCNSDP = Per capita Net State Domestic Product for respective years
2. UM NAR = Urban Male Net Attendance Ratio as per cent of total population in respective years.

3. UF NAR = Urban Female Net Attendance Ratio as per cent of total population in respective years
4. RM NAR = Rural Male Net Attendance Ratio as per cent of total population.
5. RM NAR = Rural Female Net Attendance Ratio as percent of total population.
6. TMER = Total Male Enrolment as per cent of population.
7. TFER = Total Female Enrolment as per cent of population.

III

RESULTS AND DISCUSSION

To capture the essence of human capital accumulation process, empirical growth models have concentrated on the three main levels or stages of education—primary, secondary and tertiary. Production relevant skills are assumed to be embodied to a greater extent in those individuals who have acquired greater quantity and quality of education, with a 'skills hierarchy' rising from the primary to tertiary levels (Gemmell, 1996). In simple terms the quality of workforce definitely influences economic growth. Table 4.1 shows the results of the regression explaining the relationship between NSDP and education level of the workers.

It is clear from Table 4.1 that a connection between human capital; accumulation and NSDP does exist because in the present case almost in all the cases positive and significant relationship has been detected between NSDP and level of education of the workers in primary, secondary and tertiary sectors as well. In case of the agriculture sector 34 per cent of the variations in the share of this sector in NSDP were explained by the percentage of workers having secondary level or higher education. In secondary sector this was 43 per cent and in service sector it was 46 per cent. This means that highly educated and skilled workers contribute maximum in the tertiary sector followed by secondary and primary sector.

TABLE 4.1

Net State Domestic Product (Sector-wise) and Human Capital Formation Nexus (1999-2000)

Equation No.			*Equation*				*R^2*
PRIMARY SECTOR							
1.	$NSDP_{AS}$	=	33.1 (4.98)*	+	0.215 (9.21)*	PPW	0.34
2.	$NSDP_{AS}$	=	29.31 (5.68)*	+	0.016 (7.59)*	PMW	0.22
3.	$NSDP_{AS}$	=	24.49 (6.06)*	+	0.302 (9.13)*	PSW	0.34
SECONDARY SECTOR							
4.	$NSDP_{SS}$	=	28.08 (5.57)*	+	0.23 (5.89)*	PPW	0.17
5.	$NSDP_{SS}$	=	28.8 (7.43)*	+	0.37 (7.82)*	PMW	0.27
6.	$NSDP_{SS}$	=	24.29 (5.75)*	+	0.21 (11.18)*	PSW	0.43
TERTIARY SECTOR							
7.	$NSDP_{TS}$	=	47.76 (15.15)*	+	0.25 (1.58)*	PPW	0.15
8.	$NSDP_{TS}$	=	36.68 (4.76)*	+	0.3 (5.85)*	PMW	0.26
9.	$NSDP_{TS}$	=	29.53 (7.22)*	+	0.76 (3.42)*	PSW	0.46

Note : Figures in the brackets are respective t-values.

* Significant at 1 per cent level.

Workers with primary level of education contributed maximum in agricultural sector as compared to secondary and tertiary sectors. The respective figures for R^2 are 34 per cent in agricultural sector, 17 per cent in secondary and 15 per cent in tertiary sector. This means that workers with low education contribute more in agriculture sector, because they are in the habit of putting in more physical efforts rather than mental efforts. However, all the regression coefficients except in case of tertiary sector's share in NSDP and percentage of workers having only primary education are positive and significant at one per cent level of significance. The highest value of regression coefficient among all the nine equations was 0.76 in case of tertiary sector. This suggests that one per cent increase in workers having secondary or above level of education leads to 0.76 per cent increase in tertiary sector's share in NSDP. The minimum value of regression coefficient is 0.016 in case of agriculture sector. This coefficient suggests that one per cent increase in workers with middle level of education leads to only 0.016 per cent increase in NSDP in agriculture sector.

TABLE 4.2
Wages and Human Capital Formation Nexus (1999-2000)

Equation No.			*Equation*				R^2
1.	$W_{99\text{-}00}$	=	644.84 (1.44)*	+	0.23 (5.69)*	PPW	0.3
2	$W_{99\text{-}00}$	=	1030.93 (1.62)*	+	0.23 (8.89)*	PMW	0.53
3	$W_{99\text{-}00}$	=	1619.71 (1.64)*	+	0.06 (7.82)*	PSW	0.55

Note : Figures in the brackets are respective t-values.
* Significant at 1 per cent level.

Table 4.2 shows that it is not only human capital and NSDP that are positively and significantly related to each other, rather the wages and human capital formation in the industrial sector are also positively and significantly related to each other. If the percentage of workers has secondary or higher level of education in the major industry groups of India, then 55 per cent of the total variations in their wages are explained by this variable. Fifty-three per cent of the total variation in worker's wages is explained by the workers having middle level education. Regression coefficient (i.e. 0.23) in this case suggests that one per cent increase in percentage of workers having middle level of education leads to 0.23 per cent increase in their wages. All the three regression coefficients in this case are positive and significant at one per cent level of significance, suggesting the strong and positive relationship between the two variables in the major industry of India.

Tables 4.3 through 4.6 show how per capita net state domestic product is affected by primary, middle, secondary and senior secondary education levels of males and females in rural and urban areas of various states of India. Net attendance ratio and total enrollment as per cent of total education has been used as indicators of education. The point which catches attention in both Tables 4.3 and 4.4 is the fact that all the regression coefficients are positive, though minority of them is insignificant. Urban female's education at senior secondary level is only positively and significantly associated with per capita NSDP. The correlation coefficient also in this case is .53 and .43 respectively. The next high correlation coefficient is in case of both rural and urban males at secondary level of education.

It can be observed from Tables 4.4 and 4.5 that regression coefficients are negative though insignificant in case of total enrolment of males and females for both the primary and middle level of education. This may be due to high dropout rates at primary and middle levels of education since the independent variable in this case is total enrolment ratio rather than net attendance ratio. The regression coefficients are positive and significant in case of secondary and senior secondary levels of education. Since the regression fitted is with the lag of 5 years. It is certain that after five years of completing their secondary and senior secondary level of education both male and female enter into the labour force and start contributing at micro and macro-levels. However, there is no evidence to show that returns to education in case of females and rural areas are less as compared to males and urban areas.

So the hypothesis that knowledge and skills embodied in human beings directly raise productivity in all the sectors and increase the economy's ability to grow and adopt new technologies is supported by the study. Modern agriculture is going to become bio-tech concentrated. Environmental degradation and its sustainability, safety of the workers, farm production and management, problems of land and soil, etc. need skilled and educated people to manage them. Similarly,

TABLE 4.3
Urban Attendance Ratio as Percent of Total Population in 1995-96 and Per Capita Net State Domestic Product (1993-94=00) in 2001

Sl. No.	Level of Education	Constant		Regression Coefficient	Correlation Coefficient (R)	R^2
	(1)	(2)	(3)	(4)	(5)	(6)
1.	Primary (I-V Class)	Males	10272.83 (8.15)	98.61 (0.71)	0.15	0.02
		Females	10491.36 (8.43)	43.78 (0.40	0.08	0.01
2.	Middle (VI-VIII Class)	Males	9922.93 (7.74)	284.97 (1.14)	0.23	0.05
		Females	10369.24 (8.40)	108.33 (0.62)	0.12	0.02
3.	Secondary (IX-X Class)	Males	9941.36 (8.24)	352.93 (1.36)	0.27	0.07
		Females	10424 (8.84)*	91.01 (0.67)	0.14	0.02
4.	Senior Secondary (XI-XII Class)	Males	10296.93 (8.74)*	313.79 (0.92)	0.19	0.03
		Females	9053.78 (8.31)*	1509.9 (2.99)	0.53	0.28

Note : Figures in the brackets are respective t-values.
* Significant at 5 per cent level.

TABLE 4.4
Rural Attendance Ratio as Percent of Total Population in 1995-96 and Per Capita Net State Domestic Product (1993-94=00) in 2001

Sl. No.	Level of Education		Constant	Regression Coefficient	Correlation Coefficient (R)	R^2
	(1)	(2)	(3)	(4)	(5)	(6)
1.	Primary (I-V Class)	Males	10168.25 (8.23)	135.05 (0.93)	0.19	0.04
		Females	10348.79 (8.41)	80.82 (0.66)	0.14	0.02
2.	Middle (VI-VIII Class)	Males	9985.15 (8.01)	320.95 (1.16)	0.33	0.11
		Females	9611.19 (7.84)	527.57 (1.71)	0.23	0.06
3.	Secondary (IX-X Class)	Males	9499.05 (8.06)	1363.03 (2.03)	0.39	0.15
		Females	10180.65 (8.57)	455.18 (1.07)	0.22	0.05
4.	Senior Secondary (XI-XII Class)	Males	9707.93 (7.71)	2571.27 (1.58)	0.31	0.1
		Females	9452.72 (8.26)	4425.4 (2.86)*	0.43	0.18

Note : Figures in the brackets are respective t-values.
* Significant at 5 per cent level.

TABLE 4.5
Total Enrolment as Percent of Total Population in 2000-01 and Per Capita Net State Domestic Product (1993-94=00) in 2004-05

Sl. No.	Level of Education	Constant		Regression Coefficient	Correlation Coefficient (R)	R^2
(1)	(2)	(3)	(4)	(5)	(6)	
1.	Primary (I-V Class)	Males	25047.05 (8.51)	-954.2 (- 0.65)	-0.14	0.02
		Females	25056.46 (8.38)	-825.57 (-0.62)	-0.13	0.02
2	Middle (VI-VIII Class)	Males	33375.45 (3.64)	-805.78 (- 1.05)	-0.22	0.05
		Females	30143.06 (2.39)	-544.66 (- 0.49)	-0.1	0.01
3	Secondary (IX-X Class)	Males	11328.7 (1.06)	2521.57 (1.23)	0.26	0.07
		Females	-3024.72 (- 0.36)	6157.29 (3.34)*	0.59	0.35
4	Senior Secondary (XI-XII Class)	Males	-2673.67 (0.26)	7102.02 (2.68) *	0.5	0.25
		Females	4013.08 (0.70)	690.8.67 (3.74)*	0.64	0.4

Note : Figures in the brackets are respective t-values.
* Significant at 5 per cent level.

TABLE 4.6

Total Enrolment as Per cent of Total Population in 2000-01 and Per Capita Net State Domestic Product (1993-94=00) in 2004-05

Sl. No.	Level of Education	Constant	Regression Coefficient	Correlation Coefficient (R)	R^2
	(1)	(2)	(3)	(4)	(5)
1.	Primary (I-V Class)	25103.63 (8.32)	-853.94 (- 0.64)	-0.14	0.02
2.	Middle (VI-VIII Class)	45680.53 (3.36)	-1870.56 (- 1.61)	-0.33	0.11
3.	Secondary (IX-X Class)	12199.61 (1.25)	2569.09 (1.27)	0.27	0.07
4.	Senior Secondary (XI-XII Class)	-3372.21 (-0.45)	8140.67 (3.83) *	0.64	0.41

Note : Figures in the brackets are respective t-values.
* Significant at 5 per cent level.

the growth and the performance of the industrial sector also depend not only on the quantity but also the quality of the workers. In today's liberalized regime where new products with new designs and higher performance capabilities are pouring in, unskilled labour cannot cope up with this phenomenon. Moreover, from consumer's point of view, new and high standards are being set. Particularly in food processing industries, hygiene and health safety standards are required. Similarly in agro-processing industries, especially relating to export market designing, quality, finishing, colour combination, etc. are the main requirements. Only highly skilled manpower can manage the production of these products. India's highly growing tertiary sector cannot bear the burden of unskilled and uneducated labour force. Hotel and restaurant activities, transport, communication, storage, banking, insurance, real estate, personal services, etc. require highly educated workers. Basic computer understanding for accounting, product development and designing market exploration, information gathering, etc. is required in this sector too. This is an area that can absorb many of the upcoming educated job-seekers.

It is also clear from the study that educated workers are likely to reap more financial benefits than the uneducated one; because these workers generate more value additions. Theoretical models of human capital and growth suggest some of the benefits of an educated labour force. It will generate macro-economic benefits that can't be appropriated in the form of higher earrings by those who undertake the relevant investment. These leakages are often called externalities and they provide an important rationale for education subsidies and for other policies aimed at increasing human capital investment above its 'free market' value.

On the whole, the evidence from the study is consistent with the view that measures aimed at increasing the quantity and quality of the stock of human capital should be an important part of any growth promoting policy package. Implementation of human capital policies is important for those regions or states that are lagging in productivity in NSDP, as a balanced education system promotes not only economic development but productivity. The benefits of higher education for individuals can be reaped through better employment prospects, higher salaries and greater ability to save and invest.

References

Abril, M.E.R. (2003) "Challenges and Opportunities for Gender Equality in Latin America and Caribbean", Washington D.C., World Bank.

Barro, R.J. (2001) "Human Capital and Growth," *American Economic Review*, Vol. 91, No. 2, pp. 12-17.

Centre for Monitoring Indian Economy, Various Reports.

Chadha, G.K. (2004) "Human Capital Base of the Indian Labour Market—Identifying Worry Spots", *The Indian Journal of Labour Economics*, Vol. 47, No. 1, Jan.-March, pp. 02-38.

Chen, Band and Feng, Y. (2000) "Determinants of Economic Growth in China: Private Enterprise, Education and Openers", *China Economic Review*, Vol. 11, pp. 1-15.

Chen, J. and Fleisher, B.M. (1996) "Regional Income Inequality and Economic Growth in China", *Journal of Comparative Economics*, Vol. 22, No. 2, pp. 141-64.

Denison, E.F. (1967) *Why Growth Rates Differ: Post War Experience in Nine Western Countries*, Washington, D.C., Brooking Institutions.

Fleisher, B.M. and Chen, J. (1997) "The Coast, Non-coast Income Gap, Productivity and Regional Economic Policy in India", *Journal of Comparative Economics*, Vol. 25, No. 2, pp 220-36.

Gemmell, Norman (1996) "Evaluating the Impact of Human Capital Stocks and Accumulation on Economic Growth: Some New Evidence", *Oxford Bulletin of Economics and Statistics*, (Special Issue on Human Capital in Economic Development), Vol. 58, No. 1, Feb.

Government of India (2001) *Employment and Unemployment in India, 1999-2000*, NSS Fifty Round (July 1999-June 2000), NSS Report No. 458, NSSO, May.

Government of India (2003) *National Accounts Statistics 2002*, CSO.

Lucas, R.E. (1988) "Mechanisms of Economics Growth," *Journal of Monetary Economics*, Vol. 22, pp. 3-42.

Lee (2006) "The Role of Education in Economic Growth through the Sectoral Reallocation of Labour", *Society for Economic Dynamics*, Meeting Paper No. 814.

Nelson, R.R. and E.S. Phelps (1966) "Investment in Humans Technological Diffusion and Economic Growth", *The American Economic Review*, Vol. 2, No. 56, pp. 69-75.

Schultz, T. Paul (2002) "Why Governments should Invest More to Educate Girls", *World Development*, Vol. 30, No. 2, pp. 207-25.

Schultz, Theodore, W. (1960), "Capital Formation by Education", *Journal of Political Economy*, Vol. 68, No. 6, Dec., pp. 571-83.

Wang, Y. and Y. Yao (2003) "Sources of China's Economic Growth, 1952-1999: Incorporating Human Capital Accumulation", *China Economic Review*, Vol. 14, pp. 32-52.

5

Is Investment in Women's Education Profitable?

SAILABALA DEBI

INTRODUCTION

The investment in education as an investment in human gained its importance during the 60s when T.W. Shultz (1961) for the first time highlighted the importance of education in the formation of human capital in his Presidential address in the American Economic Association. But he did not explicitly refer to the issues relating to female education. The role of women in economic development has been clearly brought out in the pioneering work of Boserup (1970). The role of women in economic development can be enhanced with education. Education of women helps them in emancipating and preparing them in playing an effective role in social, economic, political and public life. Education helps them in strengthening their human capital base in enhancing the opportunities to get better employment and hence better earning. Not only this, several research studies have also shown that returns to education of women are higher than that of men. But to many, female education is still regarded as consumption expenditure, if not a burden due to various socio-cultural factors.

In view of the importance of education of women, the paper has made an attempt to examine the profitability of investment in education of women *vis-à-vis* men. We have addressed three questions as follows:

Is investment in women's education more profitability than their men counterparts?

Which is the most profitable level/type of education for women from the point of view of households as well as the society?

In order to seek answers to the above said questions the present study makes an attempt to estimate the profitability of education in the context of a less developed region, i.e. Orissa.

The paper is divided into five sections. The second section deals briefly with the review of relevant research studies on rates of return to education. The third section attempts to estimate the average rates of return of different types and levels of education by sex and for rural and urban. The last section presents the summary of the main findings along with the concluding observations.

METHODOLOGY

The Sample and the Data

The study was based primarily on the data collected through a sample survey conducted in the district of Khurda, Orissa, as the literacy rate of the district was the highest as per the 2001 census. The sample included one urban area on the basis of literacy rate. The urban area selected for the survey was Bhubaneswar, the capital city of Orissa where not only the literacy rate is the highest but one can get different types of workers working in different sectors. We covered 253 and 249 female workers respectively working in different sectors in the city of Bhubaneswar with different types and levels of educational qualifications. The levels and types of education covered for the study are: (i) illiterates, (ii) primary, (iii) middle,

(iv) secondary, (v) general undergraduates, (vii) general graduates, (vii) general post-graduates, (viii), professional undergraduates, and (ix) professional graduates. Basic information relating to the cost and earning data and such other related information of the females and males were collected from the households and educational institutions of different types.

The Tools Used

The profitability of education is examined here through the return to their education by using the formula of Internal Rate of Return (IRR). The internal rate of return to education is defined as the rate, which equates the sum of the discounted value of benefits to the sum of discounted value of costs of education. The significance of rate of return analysis lies in the comparison of the yield of different forms of investment. Here we have compared the rate of return between different levels and types of education and between the sexes.

The formula used for IRR is as follows:

Internal Rate of Return (IRR) =

$$\sum_{t=n}^{n}[B_t/(1+r)^t] - \sum_{t=n}^{n}[C_t/(1+r)^t]$$

where B is the benefit and C is the cost of education over time period t (the period ranging from 's' to 'n', where 's' is the initial years of schooling and 'n' is the retirement age of the person), 'r' is the return.

Both the marginal and average rates of return are estimated. The average rate of return refers to the blocks of education as a whole. The average rate of return is estimated by using the above formula. The marginal rate of return, on the other hand, refers to the rate of return to additional years of education which are estimated by using the costs and earnings differentials of people between two successive levels of education.

The marginal rate of return is estimated with the help of the following formula:

$$\sum_{t=n}^{n}[B_{t\,k} - B_{tk-1}/(1+r)^t] - \sum_{t=n}^{n}[(C_{t\,k} - C_{t\,k-1})/(1+r)^t]$$

where B is the benefit and C is the cost of education over time period t (the period ranging from 's' to 'n', where 's' is the initial years of schooling and 'n' is the retirement age of the person), 'k' stands for the level of education and 'r' is the rate of return.

The rate of return is calculated here are private and social rate of return. For estimating social rate of return we have used the total resource cost (private and institutional) of education and the life time earnings of individuals before tax. For estimating the private rate of return, individual's out of pocket expenditure on education and the earnings of individual's after tax have been used. Here the earnings are considered as the benefits of the person. The direct costs and direct benefits of education are included for estimating the rate of return to different levels/types of education.

The rate of return can be divided as adjusted and unadjusted. The adjusted rate of return can be adjusted for growth of income, unemployment, ability, participation rate, wastage and stagnation, etc. Since reliable data on these variables are not easily available and many heroic assumptions need to be made for these adjustments we have not estimated the rate of return in this paper. Also for the purpose of policy-making the unadjusted rate of return is more reliable than that of adjusted rate of return. We have estimated the unadjusted rate of return in this paper.

BRIEF REVIEW OF LITERATURE ON RATE OF RETURN STUDIES

A considerable amount of research work has been done in the field of economics of educational planning in India. The rates of return studies on education in India are not very large in number. The studies on rates of return to education in India do not yield uniform results due to differences in the coverage, reference period, nature and size of data and more specifically due to differences in the methodology adopted. The study on returns to education by Harberger (1965) is claimed as a pioneering study. Nallagoudan (1967), Kothari (1967), Hussain (1967), Pandit (1972), Panchamukhi and Panchamukhi (1969), Tilak (1980) and S. Debi (1982), etc. have estimated the rates of return to education for India. Blaug, Layard and Woodhall

(1969), conducted a study to enquire into the causes of graduate unemployment in India. Chaudhury and Rao (1970), Paul (1972) etc. estimated the rate of return to certain type of professional education at the micro-level. Tilak (1980) made an attempt to estimate the rate of return to different levels of education of male and female, backward caste and non-backward castes separately at the district level. Venkat Subramanian (1980) made a similar attempt at the state level. Despite the differences in the rate of return estimates the studies provide deep insight into a number of issues. First, the theory shows that educated unemployment though important, would not affect the internal rate of return seriously. Secondly, it is pointed out that wastage and stagnation in education are quite pronounced causing a substantial fall in the rate of return. This is more in case of women students. Thirdly, the rate of return to women's education is found to be more contrary to the general belief that their rate of return is lower than males.

In so far as economics of women's education is concerned, only a very few studies on the economic analysis of women's education have so far been made in India. In Orissa, no such specific study has yet been made. The present study on the rate of return to education by sex and by region tends to be relevant for the state of Orissa from the point of view of appropriateness of educational investment allocation.

PROFITABILITY OF EDUCATION : RATES OF RETURN TO EDUCATION

The age-earnings profiles and costs of education have been used to estimate the crude/unadjusted rates of return of the sample population. In order to estimate the crude rates of return the following assumptions are made:

- There is no wastage in education.
- The secular long-term growth in incomes is assumed to be employed.
- All the students after completion of their education participate in the labour force.

- The total earnings differentials are assumed due to education alone.

All the persons live up to the end of their average working life period.

Such assumptions had to be made in view of the limitations of necessary data and also for computational advantages.

Taking into consideration the above assumptions and net earnings streams [B(benefit) – C(cost)], the internal rates of return to different types and levels of education have been calculated. The unadjusted average rates of return are estimated.

The unadjusted marginal rates of return provide a measure of effectiveness of investment in education at the margin or in other words it gives an idea about the return to additional years of schooling. Table 5.1 depicts the unadjusted marginal rate of return to different levels and types of education for both men and women are estimated both from the point of view of the

TABLE 5.1
Unadjusted Marginal Rates of Returns to Education by Sex

(in per cent)

Types/levels of education	*Private*		*Social*	
	Men	*Women*	*Men*	*Women*
E2-E1	25.79	27.05	25.15	26.13
E3-E2	22.15	23.18	20.8	21.85
E4-E3	17.18	17.89	13.61	14.08
E5-E4	15.35	15.75	12.81	13.01
E6-E4	27.83	29.33	21.16	22.1
E7-E5	14.23	15.16	11.19	12.8
E8-E7	13.88	14.09	10.95	11.0
E9-E5	12.05	12.89	10.01	10.75

Note : E1 = literate, E2 = Primary, E3 = Middle, E4 = Secondary, E5 = General undergraduate, E6 = Professional undergraduate, E7 = General graduate, E8=Professional graduate, and E9 = Prof. Grad.

individual and society in order to examine the profitability of education especially women's education. The estimates of rates of return conform to the general pattern, i.e. the rates decline as one move up the educational ladder. It may be noted that the unadjusted marginal (social and private) rates to women's education exceed those of men at every level and type of education and it increase with increase in the levels of education with exception to professional undergraduates.

The average rates of return to education give the rates of return of blocks of education as a whole. Table 5.2 presents the unadjusted average rates of return to different levels and types of education for the sample population. The average rates of return to women's education also exceed those of men at each type and level of education. The average rates of return show that next to primary education the rate of return to professional undergraduates is the highest both from private and social points of view. The average social rate of return to primary education is 16 per cent and it declined to 11 per cent for higher

TABLE 5.2

Unadjusted Average Rates of Return to Education By Sex

(in per cent)

Types/levels of education	*Rates of Return by Sex*			
	Private		*Social*	
	Private	*Social*	*Private*	*Social*
Literacy	13.6	11.61	13.65	11.82
Primary	16.69	13.13	17.01	16.05
Middle	15.27	12.81	15.80	13.01
Secondary	13.39	11.90	14.02	12.98
General undergraduates	13.00	11.02	14.89	11.93
Professional undergraduates	17.05	14.95	17.75	15.01
General graduates	12.91	10.89	13.85	11.18
Professional graduates	2.09	10.01	12.21	10.79
General post-graduates	11.83	10.08	12.27	10.87

education. The corresponding private rates are 17 per cent and 12 per cent respectively. Thus the average rates show a declining trend with an increase in educational levels for both men and women.

The reason for these higher rates of return to women's education may be largely due to lower cost and subsidized education for women/girls.

The following are the main features of rates to education estimated in the present study:

(i) The private rates of return exceed the social rates of return for both men and women.
(ii) The rates of return show a declining trend with every increase in the level of education.
(iii) The average rates of return to education for different types and levels are lower than the marginal rates of return.
(iv) The rates of return to women's education exceed those of men in both the cases, i.e., marginal and average which is due to free/subsidized/lower cost of women's education in the state. It implies that the investment in education of women is far more advantageous than investment in men's education.
(v) Women have higher relative advantage at lower levels of education as well as at professional education than their male counterparts.

SUMMARY AND CONCLUDING OBSERVATIONS

The main findings are summarized as follows:

(i) The rates of return tend to decline as one move towards higher and higher levels of education. The rates of return to primary education being the highest, the rates of return to post-graduate level is the lowest. In all the cases, i.e. for different groups of population the return to professional undergraduate level, i.e. diploma in mechanical, civil, electrical engineering, nursing, pharmacists and polytechnics, etc. shows that investment in such education is found to be the most profitable education both from the private and social points of view.

(ii) The private rate of return to education is always higher than the social rate of return.

(iii) The rates of return for women are always higher than those of men at every level/type of education.

Following the empirical findings of the study, one may be wrong in arguing that investment in education of women is consumption expenditure. The investment in education of women is as profitable as that of men. In other words, the investment in education of women is profitable (i) if it is invested in the proper level and types of education and they are allowed to participate in the labour market after education; and (ii) their education should not be used for making them eligible for the matrimonial market only but for the labour market.

References

Becker, G.S. (1962) "Investment in Human Capital: A Theoretical Analysis", *Journal of Political Economy*, Supplement, Vol. LXX, October.

Blaug, M., Layard, P.R.G. and Woodhall, M. (1969) *The Causes of Graduate Unemployment in India*, London, Penguin Press.

Bowmen, M.J. (1962b) "Social Returns to Education", *International Social Science Journal*, Vol. 14, No. 4, pp. 647-59.

Chaudhury, D.P. and Rao, P. (1970) "Private and Social Returns to Higher Education : A Case Study of Delhi Graduates", *Economic and Political Weekly*, Vol. 14, No. 5, pp. 605-08.

Debi, Sailabala. (1988) *Economics of Higher Education*, Meerut, Anu Books.

Harberger, A.C. (1965) "Investment in Men *versus* Investment in Machine: The Case of India", in C.A. Anderson and M.J. Bowmen, (eds.) *Education and Economic Development*, Chicago, Aldine, pp. 11-50.

Heyneman, S.P. (1979) "Investment in Indian Education: Uneconomic?", Staff Working Paper No. 327, Washington, D.C., World Bank.

Hussain, S.P. (1967) "Returns to Education in India", in B. Singh (ed.), pp. 141-56.

Kothari, V.N. (1967) "Returns to Education in India", in B. Singh (ed.), pp. 127-40.

Nallagounden, A.M. (1967) "Investment in Education in India", *Journal of Human Resources*, Vol. 3, No. 2, Summer, pp. 347-58.

Panchamukhi, V.R. and Panchamukhi, P.R. (1969) "Socio-economic Variables and Urban Incomes", in H.N. Pandit (ed.).

Pandit, H.N. (ed.) (1972) 'Effectiveness and Financing of Investment in Education, 1950-51 to 1965-66', Unpublished Ph.D. Thesis, Delhi University.

Paul, Samuel (1972) "An Application of Cost Benefit Analysis to Management Education", *Journal of Political Economy*, Vol. 80, No. 2 (March-April).

Psacharopoulos, G. (1969) *The Rate of Return to Investment in Education at the State of Hawaii* (Honolulu, University of Hawaii).

Psacharopoulos, G. (1973) *Returns to Education: An International Comparison*, New York, Elsevier Scientific Publishing Company.

Rogers, D. (1969) "Private Rates of Return to Education in United States: A Case Study", *Yale Economic Essay*, Vol. 9, No. 1 (Spring), pp. 89-134.

Schultz, T.W. (1961a) "Investment in Human Capital", *American Economic Review*, Vol. 51, No. 1 (March), pp. 1-17.

Tilak, Jandhyala B.G. (1980) "Inequality in the Returns to Education", Unpublished Ph.D. Dissertation, Delhi University.

World Bank (1980) "Returns to Education: An Updated International Comparison", Reprinted from G. Psacharopoulos, "Education and Income", World Bank Staff Working Paper No. 402, Washington, D.C.

6

Role of Human Capital Investment on Children's Education : A Study on Rural Households in Tamil Nadu

E. Nanda Kumar and A. Sangamithra

INTRODUCTION

In the early 20th Century, Marshall emphasised that "the most valuable of all capital is that investment on human beings" and that "knowledge is our most powerful engine of production; it enables us to subdue nature and force to satisfy our wants". According to the human capital theory, education transforms raw human beings into productive 'Human Capital' by imparting knowledge and improving skills required by both the traditional and modern sector of the economy, and makes individual more productive members of the society, not only in the market place but also in the households and also in the whole society. Human capital is also defined as the stock of skills and productive knowledge embodied in people.(Rosen, 1987). In economics, capital is defined as a factor of production which helps to enlarge productive potential of the society. Human being is a capital asset, which yields a series of economic benefits over his working life. It is a part of man (Schultz, 1971). It is "Human" because it is embodied in man and it is "Capital" because it is a source of future satisfaction or earning or both. Human capital, unlike other physical assets, cannot be sold but can be acquired by means of investing in oneself. Investment in human capital includes all activities that increase human resources (Nickell *et. al.*, 1976). Expenditure on human resource and development came to be regarded as an investment (Dhingra, 1988). It seems to be perceived as a process of contributing to and developing of the quality embodied in human beings (Mathur, 1981).

INVESTMENT IN EDUCATION AND ECONOMIC GROWTH

The role of education in social and economic development, in reducing poverty and inequality, as a possible contributor to greater social and economic equality and as an enhancer of development was widely recognized from the days of Adam Smith. Education represents both consumption and investment. On the one hand, it is valued for its immediate benefits; while on the other it helps to create income in the future by endowing workers with skill and knowledge that enable them to increase their productive capacities. Expenditure on education is a valuable investment. Education matters for economic growth, reduction in poverty and inequalities, and improvement in income distribution, besides contributing to other social, political and cultural dimensions of development and human development. From a narrow point of view of economic returns, there is sufficient justification for public funding on education in comparison with other economic sectors.

Investment in human capital is widely viewed as the expenditure on education, health, training, career-related knowledge and skills which improve the productive capacity of the person, increase his adaptability to the changing requirements of the economy, improves the quality of human beings and increase the future income potential of a person, family and the nation at large. Does investment in education necessarily enhance economic growth? There are compelling reasons that it should, but the empirical evidence does not always support this conclusion. Individuals are willing to take more years of schooling partly because they can earn more and get better jobs. For many, more schooling can also be a source of social mobility.

The link between education and economic growth in some of the early works was based on the argument that a major effect of more education is that an improved labor force has an increased capacity to produce. As better-educated workers are more literate and numerate, it is easier to train them and they can learn more complex tasks. In addition, they usually have better work habits.

INTRA-HOUSEHOLD ASPECTS OF HUMAN CAPITAL INVESTMENT

Where does human capital come from? What constitutes a successful investment in human capital, either at the individual or national level? One has to start with the household which is the foundation of a good society and of economic success. Households have differed over time, but they are still very important in the modern economy. To understand human capital, we have to go back to the household, because it is the families that are concerned about children and try with whatever resources they have to promote their children's education and values. Households are the major promoters of values in a free society and even in not-so-free societies. Rogers (1990) defined the household as not an undifferentiated unit, but "an economy in microcosm, a system of exchanges, entitlements, and responsibilities allocated among members in a group whose boundaries are far from clear". Gary, S. Becker (1933) in his book: *A Treatise on the Family* identified the parental role in developing the human capital of children. The investment in children's human capital, under credit constraints, necessarily entails foregone current consumption for the household. There are two innovations in Becker approach, pertaining to the theory and to the empirical testing, (i) Parental decision to invest in children's human capital motivated by the returns that will accrue not only to the children, but also the portion of the returns that will generate transfers to parents in future, and (ii) Use the intra-household resource allocation approach to investigate the present costs (foregone consumption) and future benefits of these investment, in children.

Family is an institution. In spite of the revolutionary changes in science, technology and structure of the economy values of family continue to be important. Given the large fraction of life one spends in a family sharing resources and expenditures, the distribution of welfare among members of society depends to a large extent on the distribution of resources among families, and most development objectives focus on the well-being of individuals. Individual endowments are not merely genetic; investing in human capital can argument the needs, activities and characteristics of members. It is widely accepted that one of the important functions of family as social institution is the building of human capital of children in the form of education.

NEED FOR THE STUDY

Human capital is by all counts the most crucial factor in the process of economic development. Investment in Human Capital includes investment in education, health and nutrition. For an accelerated economic development it is necessary that not only physical but also the human capital is accumulated at a high rate. In the present state of technological advancement it is absolutely essential to regard education and training as the most potential ingredients of capital. Actually, education is now being regarded as the first investment in existing human capital. Evidence in economics strengthens the view that promoting human welfare need, among the other things, investment in people in the form of education. It is necessary for individuals as well as national development and welfare that such investments in children or people take place. Even though education is available at a much subsidized rate, children do not get education to the extent they should. When one tries to understand the reason behind this, it reveals that it is the individual household which plays crucial role for such investment. In order to understand the factors that influence investment in children it becomes necessary to understand the family/household decision-making process and more especially the allocation of resources for children's education.

Of late, the allocation of resources within the household has become an important issue of research. Within the given income resource allocation among the family members has caught the attention of social scientists. Gender discrimination for allocating resources for children's education has been an important area of research. Household is a place where responsibilities are allocated according to ability and resources are allocated according to need. One thing common among all the people in the world is that they belong to one or the other household. It has been recognized that the household is the important component of an economy and many activities take place in the household sector. Therefore, the present study is undertaken.

OBJECTIVES OF THE STUDY

The following are the objectives of the study:

- To study the socio-economic conditions of the rural households.
- To analyse the pattern of investment in education of rural children.
- To analyse the presence or absence of gender discrimination among the sample respondents of rural households.

DATA SOURCES AND METHODOLOGY

To achieve the above objectives primary data were collected from the rural households of Kinathukadavu Block in

Coimbatore District, Tamil Nadu. Based on the different income groups, 142 rural households were selected at random and the pattern of investment and gender discrimination on human capital investment on children's education were analysed with the help of mean, standard deviation and Ordinary Least Squares and Stepwise Regression Method.

ANALYSIS OF THE DATA

The collected data have been analyzed by using Ordinary Least Squares (OLS) and Stepwise Regression Method. To analyze the empirical work we use regression analysis. It is used in this analysis because it would explain parental role in developing human capital of children. In other words, it would explain the determinants of volume of expenditure incurred by the parents on the education of children. In this study the dependent variable is a continuous variable. The independent variables, such as occupation of father or mother and education of father and mother are dichotomous or categorical variables in the regression and are treated as 'dummies'. Therefore, our basic model is Ordinary Least Squares (OLS) regression with continuous and dummy regressors.

$$E.EDU = a_1 + \sum_{i=1}^{n} b_1 Xij + U_1$$

where E.EDU are the dependent variables,

E.EDU stands for Education expenditure on children,

i : stands for independent variable,

j : stands for individual child,

Xij : (I = 1.........n) are the independent variables continuous or dummy variables, and

U_1 and U_2 are unobserved random variables.

Specifically the model hypothesized that the parental role of investment in human capital (i.e.) expenditure on education is a function of total monthly income of the family, age of father, age of mother, education of father and mother, size of the family, occupation of head of the family.

TABLE 6.1
Regression Results of Expenditure on Education of Children

Variables	*Equation 1*	*Equation 2*	*Equation 3*
Constant	3.432 (51.38)	3.248 (37.41)	2.725 (12.57)
Total Monthly Income	0.53 (7.207)*	0.406 (5.014)*	0.354 (4.333)*
Age of Father (in years)	0.16 (2.157)**	0.188 (2.621)***	—
Age of Mother (in years)	0.138 (1.84)	0.169 (2.33)	0.038 (0.29)
Education of the Father (in years)	0.258 (3.181)**	—	0.281 (3.520)*
Education of the Mother (in years)	0.169 (2.097)***	0.024 -.235	0.076 -.758
Total size of the family	0.011 (0.16)	0.044 (0.61)	0.037 (0.53)
Occupation of the family head	0.003 (0.03)	-.046 (-.602)	-.035 (-.461)
R Square	0.281	0.332	0.365
F	51.94	32.812	25.137

* 1% Level of Significance.
** 5% Level of Significance.
*** 10% Level of Significance.

RESULTS AND DISCUSSION

The first equation of Table 6.1 shows that the total monthly income, age of father, education of father and mother have emerged significant on investment of education for their children. The model shows that income is the important determinant for investment in education with one per cent level of significance. Higher the income more will be the investment on education. Age of the father shows five percent level of significance which indicates that with increase in the age of the father, more funds are allocated on the education of children.

Education of the father is also important for investing in education of children. If the father is well educated, he invests more on his children's education. Likewise, mother's education also influences the investment in children's education with 10 per cent level of significance. This model shows only 28 per cent of variation in household expenditure on education.

The second equation of Table 6.1 reveals that total monthly income and age of the father are statistically significant. Total monthly income shows one per cent level of significance where it indicates that higher family income brings increasing household investment in children's education. Similarly, age of the father shows 10 per cent level of significance because the age of father is considered important in the context of investing in education of their children. This model explains variation by about 33 per cent.

Equation 3 shows that total monthly income and education of father are statistically significant shows at 1 per cent level of significance. All the three models show that income is significant to the investment on education of children. Education of father has influenced the investment on education of children. Higher levels of education of father reflects both the greater and efficiency in the production of human capital and a better perception of the returns to schooling for the children, educated father tends to provide better schooling for their children than a less educated fathers.

GENDER DISCRIMINATION OF CHILDREN

The Governments all over the world have taken various measures to bridge the gap between gender variations. But this disparity still exists in many countries including India. Gender discrimination with regard to human capital investment is no exception. Gender discrimination in education directly affects economic growth by lowering the average level of human capital. Education of women benefits individuals, families and communities. By educating women, a country can reduce poverty, improved productivity, ease population pressure and offer its children a better future. A number of studies have shown that economic and social returns to the family as a result of education for women are greater than those for men.

Educated parents have better educated children and maternal education tends to influence a girl's education in particular.

The differential treatment of children at household level based on gender is a much talked about subject in social science disciplines. Since we have ventured to study the household resource allocation in education, it is imperative to look into the discrimination if any in the expenditure on education of boys and girls. Based on the mean we have attempted to analyze the gender discrimination between the boy and girl in the rural households. Based on the expenditure made by the parents for both of their children we have calculated mean and standard deviation and co-efficient of variation for education.

In Table 6.2, the results show the extent of mean expenditures spent on the boy and girl child for their education. The mean educational expenditure made on the male child is Rs. 615.42 whereas in case of female child they spent fewer amounts on the education of female child that is Rs. 587.50. Educational expenditure for male child is more than the female child. This implies that there is a need for treating equally to girls and boys. This is likely to increase the enrolment of girls in schools and colleges.

TABLE 6.2
Mean and Standard Deviation for the Amount Spent on Education between Male and Female Child

Expenditure	*Mean*	*Std. Dev.*	*C.V. (In Rs.)*
Male	615.42	633.098	97.21
Female	587.50	970.640	60.53

CONCLUSION

Education serves to develop individuals to become competent and responsible citizens. It gives men and women an opportunity to acquire understanding of the values and philosophy of life (Swanson, 1981). Children included several aspects such as provision of various facilities, providing motivation, guidance, supervision and participation of the parents in educational activities. Economic literature has shown that schooling is an engine of growth, but schooling is at best a weak proxy of all human capital.

Household economic theory views that future welfare of the child enters the consumption function of the parent through investment in child's education. Educational qualification of the father also greatly influences investment in education. Higher level of education of parents plays a predominant role in the production of human capital and a better perception of the returns to schooling for the children, Educated father tends to provide better schooling for his children as compared to the less educated. It is established that, by and large, parents try to educate their children to a level higher than what they have attained. Hence, they allocate more resources on children's education.

The results show that most of the families are sending their children to private schools in order to get better education. One-fourth of households prefer government schools because of their low income. They are not in a position to invest more on their children's education. Further, educational expenditure for male child is more than the female child. This implies that there is a need for awareness among the parents to invest more on the education of female child and treating the girls and boys equally. This will result in higher enrolment of girl children in schools and colleges. Education can be an important instrument to reduce gender discrimination.

References

Becker, G.S. (1964) "Human Capital: A Theoretical and Empirical Analysis, With Special Reference to Education", New York, Columbia University Press.

Bouchard, P. (1998) "Training and Work: Myths about Human Capital", Toronto, Thompson Educational Publishing Co.

Blaugh, M. (1976) "The Empirical Status of Human Capital Theory: A Slightly Jaundiced Survey", *Journal of Economic Literature,* 14.

Dipankar, Purkayastha (2003) "From Parents to Children: Intra-household Altruism at Institutional Behaviour", *Journal of Economic Issues,* Vol. XXXVII, No. 3, September.

Duncan, Thomas (1991) "Gender Differences in Household Resource Allocation", Living Standards Measurement Study, Working paper No. 79, Washington, World Bank.

Psacharopoulos, George (1987) *Education Research and Studies*, Pergamon Press.

Illhan, Ozturk (2001) "The Role of Education in Economic Development: A Theoretical Perspective", *Journal of Rural Development and Administration*, Vol. XXXIII, No. 1, Winter, pp. 39-47.

Kaur, Kuldip (2008) "Education, Growth and Wages in India—An Inter-relationship", *91st Annual Conference Volume*, Indian Economic Association, December.

Kiker, B.F. (1967) "The Concept of Human Capital in the History of Economic Thought", *The Indian Economic Journal*, Vol. XIV.

Mark, Schonewille (2001) "Does Training Make a Difference? Institutional Environment and Returns to Human Capital", Paper for the International Labour Market Conference at Aberdeen, University of Nijmegan.

Martin, Husz (1998) "Human Capital, Endogenous Growth, and Government Policy", Peter Lang Gmbh.

Meeneesha, Shukul (2007) "Investment in Human Capital by Families," *Journal of Social Sciences*, 14(2).

Nagapal, C.S. and Mittal, A.C. (1963) "Education for Economic and Social Development", in *Economics of Education*, New Delhi, Anmol Publication.

Schultz, Paul T. (1992) "The Role of Education and Human Capital in Economic Development: An Empirical Assessment", Paper Presented at the Conference on Economic Growth in the World Economy.

Brown, Philip H. (2006) "Parental Education and Investment in Children's Human Capital in Rural China", *Economic Development and Cultural Change*, Vol. 54.

Rubenson, K. (1992), "Human Resource Development: A Historical Perspective", in L.E. Burton, In *Developing Resourceful Humans: Adult Education within the Economic Context*, New York, Routledge.

Schultz, T.W. (1961) "Investment in Human Capital", *The American Economic Review*, pp. 1-17.

Tilak, J.B.G. (2008), "Education, Growth and Development", *91st Annual Conference Volume*, Indian Economic Association, December.

Yueh, L.Y. (2001) "A Model of Parental Investment in Children's Human Capital", Skope Research Paper No. 15, Spring, University of Oxford.

7

Level of Education and Employment in Punjab

HARVINDER KAUR

INTRODUCTION

Punjab, once the most prosperous state of the country, has been lagging far behind in terms of per capita income since 1993-94. Being primarily an agro-based economy, the state has also lagged in economic growth on account of slowdown in agriculture sector. At the same time, the growth of secondary sector, especially of manufacturing sector has not been of satisfactory level. The service sector, however, is emerging as a fast growing sector of the economy of Punjab and constitutes over 40 per cent of Net State Domestic Product (NSDP). Though this sector has bypassed the industrial sector, yet industrialisation remains a pre-requisite for growth. For the sake of sustainable growth, industrialisation should not have been bypassed (*Asian Development Outlook*, 2007). As a result, a shift in the workforce from agriculture to non-agriculture sector is taking place. Agriculture sector accounted for 62.66 per cent and non-agriculture sector 37.34 per cent of the total workforce in 1971. Now the picture has almost reversed. As per the 2001 Census, about 39 per cent of the working population of the state is employed in agriculture sector and 61 per cent in the non-agriculture sector.

Sectoral shifts towards non-agricultural sector, thus, require more educated and skilled workers. No doubt, the number of recognised educational institutions (like schools, colleges specifically engineering colleges, and universities) and the number of students have been increasing. These institutions ironically remain under-staffed affecting the quality of learning. Consequently, the pupil-teacher ratio has been increasing. This ratio was 43:1 at the primary stage, 28:1 at middle level and 26:1 at high/senior stage in 2006. There is, therefore, an urgent need to employ more teachers in these institutions.

No doubt, literacy rate has been improving, but what irks the economists is the 16th rank that the state holds amongst 28 states and 7 UTs. Further, the picture regarding level of education of people in Punjab is very disappointing. Among the literates, a little less than half (44 per cent) are those who have below-primary or primary level of education, and a little more than one-fifth (22 per cent) are matriculates. The proportion of those holding graduation degree or higher is a mere 6.6 per cent. Interestingly, this proportion is also higher among females (6.7 per cent) than the males (6.4). This reflects the low level of education in Punjab leading to a lack in high and middle level manpower development. Four decades back economists from industrialised countries cautioned about the occurrence of major bottlenecks in economic growth in non-industrial countries, because of lack of high and middle level manpower (Carnoy, 1977).

Educated and trained manpower is one of the major inputs for economic and social development. Thus, the co-ordination between educational planning and manpower planning is seen as one of the solutions to the problem of sustainable economic growth. The important question which arises is the economic condition of the state deteriorating due to a lack of vision of the Central and state governments? Why no serious attention is being paid towards the development of human capital in accordance with the changing needs? In the present paper an attempt has been made to analyse the educational level of workers, pattern of employment, and expenditure on education during the Annual Plans of Punjab.

II

LITERACY RATE, WORK PARTICIPATION RATE, AND EDUCATIONAL LEVEL OF WORKERS IN PUNJAB

Establishing a close relationship between education and work has been a top priority in the developed countries. However, such an effort is lacking in the developing countries. In India a reference to the connection between education and employment has been made in the Eleventh Five Year Plan (2007-12). The role of education in facilitating social and economic progress is well recognised in the Plan. According to it, "Education is the most crucial input for empowering people with skills and knowledge and giving them access to productive employment in future". The need for the adaptation of education to generate employment, however, still remains neglected.

Punjab is well-known for its energetic people. Efforts to equip this energetic community with education are giving significant results. Table 7.1 reveals that the literacy rate in Punjab has almost doubled during the last three decades, from 33.67 per cent to 69.7 per cent. According to Census 2001, Punjab has 147.56 lakh literates. Among them 84.42 lakh are males and 63.14 lakh are females. The state has also 94.35 lakh illiterates. Female literacy rate in the state has increased from 24.65 per cent in 1971 to 63.35 per cent in 2001 as compared to the male literacy rate which increased from 42.23 per cent to 75.2 per cent during 1971 to 2001. The rise in female literacy rate in the state during this period is higher by 10 percentage points as compared to the rise in female literacy rate at the national level.

The state has also shown a marked improvement in the work participation rate, which has increased from 28.87 per cent in 1971 to 37.58 per cent in 2001. However, it still remains marginally lower than the national level (39.26 per cent). Female

TABLE 7.1
Literacy Rate and Work Participation Rate in Punjab and India

		1971	*1981*	*1991*	*2001*	*Increase 1971-2001*
			Punjab			
Literacy Rate	P	34.12	43.37	58.51	69.95	35.83
	M	42.23	51.23	65.66	75.63	34.40
	F	24.65	34.35	50.41	63.55	38.90
Work	P	28.87	31.50	30.88	37.58	8.71
Participation	M	52.82	53.76	54.22	54.10	1.28
Rate	F	1.18	6.16	6.78	18.68	17.50
			India			
Literacy Rate	P	34.45	43.56	52.21	64.84	30.39
	M	45.95	56.37	64.13	75.26	29.31
	F	21.97	29.75	39.29	53.67	32.30
Work	P	33.08	36.70	37.50	39.26	6.18
Participation	M	52.61	52.62	51.61	51.93	-0.68
Rate	F	12.11	19.67	22.27	25.68	13.57

work participation has surged from 1.18 per cent in 1971 to 18.68 per cent in 2001. But it is lower than the national female work participation rate by 7 percentage points. Gender gap in literacy rate has come down from 17.58 percentage points in 1971 to 12.08 percentage points in 2001 and in work participation rate it has fallen from 51.64 percentage points to 35.42 percentage points in 2001. The figures indicate that the gap in the literacy rate between the sexes is not wide, but a higher gap in the work participation rate is visible. It clearly reflects from the data that the higher the literacy rate the higher is the work participation rate. The issue which needs to be addressed is the enhancement of female work participation in Punjab.

As the educational level of workers affects their efficiency and productivity, it is important to analyse the same with respect to the state. Table 7.2 presents the percentage of main

TABLE 7.2
Percentage of Main Workers and Marginal Workers by Sex and Educational Level in Punjab

	1981				1991			
	Main Workers		*Marginal Workers*		*Main Workers*		*Marginal Workers*	
	M	*F*	*M*	*F*	*M*	*F*	*M*	*F*
(1)	(2)	(3)	(4)	(5)	(6)	(7)	(8)	(9)
Illiterate	52.6	50.9	52.6	84.7	41.4	44.2	50.1	73.9
Literate								
without education	4.8	1.8	5.96	2.45	3.96	2.2	5.8	2.5
Primary	13.6	5.2	15.1	1.1	14.5	7.1	15.8	12.6
Middle	10.7	2.8	9.9	2.0	12.6	4.0	10.97	4.8
Matriculation/Secondary	11.8	11.2	10.9	1.5	18.98	13.6	12.4	5.3
Under graduation	2.6	4.3	2.3	0.2	3.8	4.1	2.5	0.4
Graduation	2.5	6.04	2.3	0.16	5.1	18.3	1.7	0.4
Post-Graduate	0.4	2.3	0.07	0.01				

(*Contd.*)

TABLE 7.2 (Contd.)

(1)	(2)	(3)	(4)	(5)	(6)	(7)	(8)	(9)
Technical/ Certificate/degree/ diploma post-graduate	1.0	15.3	0.95	0.1	0.6	6.6	0.8	0.17
Total	100 (4749646)	100 (178113)	100 (54698)	100 (305454)	5832852	265522	10491	153124

Sources : Computed from data available in:
(i) Census of India, 1981, Series 17, Punjab, Part-IIIA and B, Vol. I (General Economic Tables).
(ii) Census of India, 1991, Series 20, Punjab, Part-IIIB, Economic Tables.

workers and marginal workers according to their sex and educational level in Punjab. A large number of main as well as marginal workers, both male and female, are illiterate. However, this has witnessed a significant downward trend. The percentage of illiterate male main workers declined from 52.6 per cent to 41.4 per cent during 1981 and 1991 and that of illiterate male marginal workers came down from 52.6 per cent to 50.1 per cent. Similarly, the percentage of illiterate female main workers and marginal workers has declined from 50.9 to 44.2 and 84.7 to 73.9 respectively during 1981 and 1991. Comparatively, a higher percentage of female workers—main as well as marginal—are illiterate. The percentage of female workers having primary, middle and matriculation level of education is lower than that of male workers having the same level of education. The situation gets reversed subsequently at higher levels of education. The percentage of female main workers having post-secondary, graduation, post-graduation and certificate/degree/diploma and post-graduate level technical education is higher than that of male main workers. Now, we can well imagine that how a state, where only 10 per cent of male main workers and only 30 per cent female main workers having a level of education above matriculation (in 1991) can make the desired progress. There is, therefore, a need to upgrade the education and skill level of the existing as well as potential workers.

III

NATURE OF EMPLOYMENT IN PUNJAB

An overwhelming majority, i.e. more than 90 per cent of the workers are employed in the unorganised sector in Punjab. In 1981 and 1991, the percentage of workers in the organised sector was 12 and 12.9 respectively, which was further reduced to 9.2 in 2001. Table 7.3 reveals the position of employment in the organised sector in Punjab. Employment in the organised sector (public and private) has been continuously declining since 2004. Of the total organised employment, a total of 439,073 (59.35 per cent) employees work in public sector, and the remaining 300,679 (40.65 per cent) work in private sector as on 31st March, 2007.

Table 7.3
Employment in the Organised Sector in Punjab (Public and Private Sector)

	1981	1991	2001	2002	2003	2004	2005	2006	2007
(1)	*(2)*	*(3)*	*(4)*	*(5)*	*(6)*	*(7)*	*(8)*	*(9)*	*(10)*
I. Public Sector									
(i) Central Government	67,460	72,308	79,198	75,000	70,000	71,238	70,150	68,036	67,037
(ii) State Government	2,55,505	2,93,577	3,02,124	3,02,000	2,96,000	2,89,718	2,66,854	2,91,076	2,57,949
(iii) Quasi Government	1,16,606	1,71,618	1,73,548	1,74,000	1,61,000	1,70,517	1,53,138	1,66,599	87,140
(iv) Local Government	28,224	32,556	31,276	30,000	29,000	33,132	29,834	29,722	26,916
Total (I)	4,67,795	5,70,059	5,86,164	5,81,000	56,000	5,64,605	5,19,976	4,22,460	4,39,073
II. Private Sector	1,67,340	2,21,230	2,61,083	2,55,000	2,44,000	2,61,339	2,53,104	2,76,290	3,00,679
Grand Total I and II	6,35,135	7,91,289	8,47,247	8,36,000	8,00,000	8,25,944	7,73,116	7,68,750	7,39,752

Source : Government of Punjab, *Economic Survey of Punjab* (Various issues).

Punjab's labour force is growing at a rate higher than the rate of growth of employment. The population of the state has increased from 135,51060 in 1971 to 2,43,58999 in 2001. In percentage terms, the state has been registering a decadal growth rate of more than 20 per cent since 1971. Work participation rate, on the other hand, has grown from 28.87 per cent in 1971 to 37.58 per cent in 2001 i.e. by 8.71 percentage points only. The magnitude of unemployment continues to be a cause of serious concern in Punjab (*Economic Survey of Punjab*, 2007-08). There is an acute shortage of 1.32 lakh personnel in various government departments. (*The Tribune*, Sept. 5, 2008). On the one hand the government is not inclined to fill up the vacancies and create new jobs and on the other hand, new employment opportunities in the unorganised sector have not been able to keep pace with the growth in the labour force. The number of work seekers on the live register of employment exchanges was 442,225 (as on 31st March 2007). Among them, 75,494 were technical personnel and 232,953 were non-technical fresher educated.

After the agriculture and IT revolution, an industrial revolution in Punjab is overdue. The industrial sector contributes a low share in GSDP. Its contribution is less than 15 per cent of the Gross State Domestic Product for the state during 2006-07. The tertiary sector has been contributing more than 40 per cent, while the secondary sector has been contributing 20 to 25 per cent in GSDP since 2001. It shows that growth in the service sector has by-passed the growth in the industrial sector. Development of industry, mainly through development of agro-based and manufacturing units, can revive and accelerate the growth rate of the economy. Large and medium units have greater potentiality to absorb technically trained and skilled manpower. The solution to optimum utilisation of human resources and rapid economic growth of Punjab economy lies in the balanced growth of three sectors: the increase in the formation of physical capital, industrialisation, and investment in education. More capital and industries would create jobs and more education and improved skill would make the population efficient, productive and more employable. All this, in turn, would increase income, standard of living, and economic growth.

Table 7.4
Expenditure on Education in Punjab

(*Lakh rupees*)

Year	*General Education*		*Technical Education*		*Social Services*	
	Actual Exp.	*% to total Exp.*	*Actual Exp.*	*% to total Exp.*	*Actual Exp.*	*% to total Exp.*
(1)	(2)	(3)	(4)	(5)	(6)	(7)
1980-81*	626.60	2.09	15.01	0.05	5,858.36	19.56
1989-90*	2,115.27	2.43	505.17	0.58	16,461.26	18.94
1992-93	1,761.90	1.99	2,556.88	2.88	20,942.10	23.62
1993-94	3,886.75	3.40	2,833.98	2.48	30,560.00	26.74
1994-95	5,312.97	3.86	3,873.10	2.82	37,479.73	27.26
1995-96	5,130.23	3.23	4,141.50	2.61	32,587.17	20.54
1997-98	9,879.21	4.91	3,073.16	1.53	41,419.57	20.59
1998-99	15,582.50	7.7	2,677.70	1.34	45,399.17	22.65
1999-2000	18,224.86	10.40	4,363.04	2.49	63,003.35	35.94
2001-02	20,414.92	10.22	1,085.72	0.54	69,390.29	34.29
2002-03	4,805.19	2.42	463.83	0.23	50,439.43	25.44
2003-04	6,237.66	3.92	203.48	0.12	38,84.69	24.19
2004-05	10,227.07	5.2	216.67	0.11	33,911.18	17.32
2005-06	15,549.30	4.14	278.80	0.07	1,01813.77	27.12
2006-07	24,095.95	5.82	457.33	0.11	1,09374.72	26.41
2007-08*	37,334.39	7.30	2,655.00	0.52	1,58747.66	31.06

• Social and Community Services, Approved outlay.
Source : *Statistical Abstract of Punjab* (Various Issues).

IV

PUBLIC EXPENDITURE ON EDUCATION IN PUNJAB

As the issue of human resource development has been gaining momentum, the Centre and the state governments are increasing expenditure on social sector, particularly on education and training. So far as Punjab is concerned, it shows a dismal picture. Actual expenditure on education in various Annual Plans of Punjab is shown in Table 7.4.

The figures reveal that actual expenditure on general education as a percentage of total expenditure continuously increased from 2.09 per cent in 1980-81 to 10.2 per cent in 2001-02. Thereafter, it has varied between 2 to 6 per cent. Similarly, actual expenditure on technical education as a percentage of total expenditure reached 2.5 per cent in 1999-2000 from 0.05 per cent in 1980-81. But thereafter, instead of increase in percentage of expenditure on technical education, which is in high demand and directly related to employment, it has declined to the level of less than one per cent of total expenditure. It is thus clear that there is a lack of co-ordination between education and manpower planning and there is need to link educational planning to the emerging needs of the labour market in Punjab.

V

SUMMARY

The state of Punjab can, no doubt, be included in the economically advanced regions of India. But it has lost the glory of once being the topper in terms of per capita income. It has lagged behind in terms of economic growth. Slowdown of agriculture sector, unsatisfactory growth of manufacturing sector and fast growth of tertiary sector has changed the entire structure of the economy. This has resulted in sectoral shifts. Workforce is shifting from agriculture to non-agricultural sector. To increase the productivity in agriculture sector and to meet the needs of the secondary and tertiary sectors, more educated and skilled workers are required. No doubt, literacy rate has been continuously improving, but level of education is very low in Punjab. Only less than one-third of the literate people have educational level of matric and above. How can a region grow which lacks high and middle level manpower! Work participation rate has been improving, but a very low educational level of workers is a cause to worry. In Punjab about 40 to 50 per cent of the workforce is illiterate. Besides this, more than 90 per cent of those who are working in the unorganised sector are paid low wages. The organised sector is shrinking and new employment opportunities in the unorganised sector are not growing at a rate commensurate with the growth rate of the labour force. As a result, unemployment has become a serious problem causing social and personal unrest. The above discussion leads to the conclusion that neither human resources are fully developed nor fully utilised in the state. Education and manpower planning does not receive top priority by the state government. Expenditure on general education as per cent of total expenditure, after reaching at 10.2 per cent in 2001-02, has plummeted to between 2 to 6 per cent. Similarly, actual expenditure on technical education has declined to less than one per cent of the total expenditure. Apathetic approach of the government towards co-ordination between education planning and manpower planning will push the economy towards further deceleration.

References

Asian Development Outlook 2007.

Carnoy, Martin (1977), *Education and Employment: A Critical Appraisal,* Paris, Unesco, Government of Punjab. *Economic Survey of Punjab, 2007-08.*

Government of India, *Eleventh Five Year Plan 2007-12,* Vol. II, New Delhi, Government of India, Planning Commission.

Government of Punjab, *Human Development Report of Punjab, 2004.*

8

Growth of Engineering and Technical Education in India : Causes and Patterns

PRADEEP KUMAR CHOUDHURY

INTRODUCTION

The significant growth of higher education in India has contributed to the building up of the third largest reservoir of scientific and technical professional manpower in the world. This has helped the nation in achieving a reasonably high and sustainable rate of economic growth and in the realization of the national goal of self-reliance in various sectors. From the global point of view it has also been well-recognized that India supplies highly skilled scientific and technical manpower to the world market produced at a relatively lower cost (Tilak, 1985).

At the same time, it should be noted that, despite the massive absolute growth in the number of institutions and enrolments, there are only 72 people getting engineering education per lakh population. Further, the present technical education system of the country is not able to keep pace with the industrial development and technological advancement. The requirement of technical education in future will be different both in intentions and executions in comparison to that of today. Hence, there is an urgency to change India's present policy of technical education accordingly.

Against this backdrop, the present paper will focus on the growth and pattern of engineering education in India during the last four decades. The whole paper has been structured in the following manner. The First Section presents an overall picture of engineering education in the pre-independence period. Section II analyzes the situation in the post-independence period. Emerging issues and concerns in engineering education in India have been explained in the Third Section of the paper. The structural stability between per capita income and the enrolment in engineering education has been explained in the Fourth Section with the help of Chow test. Finally, the paper ends with a brief conclusion which is almost a summary of the whole paper.

ENGINEERING INSTITUTIONS IN PRE-INDEPENDENCE SCENARIO

In 1847, the first engineering college was established in Roorkee named as Thomson Engineering College to train civil engineers. Before this, there were some industrial schools in Calcutta and Bombay which were attached to the ordinance factories and other engineering establishments. However, the first formal school for engineering was set-up in Guindy, Madras, in 1842, which was attached to the Gun carriage factory there. Further in 1854, a school for training the overseers was established in Poona. In this phase, the Britishers realized the need for creating such schools of engineering and training for overseers for the construction and maintenance of public buildings, roads, canals and ports. In 1856, the Calcutta College of Civil Engineering was opened and in 1858 the overseers school of Poona was renamed as Poona Engineering College and was affiliated to Bombay University. Similarly, the industrial school in Madras was renamed as Guindy College of Engineering, affiliated to University of Madras.

A similar pattern of educational process was followed in all the three colleges of Calcutta, Poona and Guindy. They all had licentiate courses in civil engineering up to 1880 and organized degree classes in this branch alone. After 1880, the demand for mechanical and electrical engineering was felt, but the three Engineering Colleges started only apprenticeship classes in these subjects. The Victoria Jubilee Technical Institute, which was started in Bombay in 1887 had its objective to train licentiates in electrical, mechanical and textile engineering. In 1907 the leaders of the Swadeshi Movement organized a National Council of Education in West Bengal, and opened many institutions. Out of the many institutions it started, only the College of Engineering and Technology at Jadavpur had survived. It started granting diplomas in mechanical and engineering course in 1908 and in chemical engineering in 1921. In 1915 the Indian Institute of Science, Bangalore, started teaching in electrical engineering. Likewise a few engineering colleges were started in selected places of India in the pre-independence era.

ENGINEERING INSTITUTIONS IN POST-INDEPENDENCE PERIOD

Quite a number of engineering colleges have been started since 1947 in India. It is due to the realization that India has to become a great industrial country and would require a far larger number of engineers than could be supplied by the older institutions. In some cases, existing lower type institutions have been raised to the status of degree-giving colleges. In 1945, the Sarkar Committee was appointed to suggest options for advanced technical education in India. This Committee recommended the establishment of higher technical institutes based on the Massachusetts Institute of Technology in four regions of India. This resulted in the setting up of five Indian Institutes of Technology at Kharagpur (1950), Bombay (1958), Kanpur (1959), Madras (1960), and Delhi (1961). The All India Council of Technical Education (AICTE) was established to advise on improvement and development of technical education in India. Another important step taken after independence was the appointment of a Scientific Manpower Committee to assess the requirements of various categories of scientific and technical manpower for the country. Since Independence there has been a significant increase in the number of engineering institutions and student's enrolment. Figure 8.1 shows the number of engineering institutions in different periods and Table 8.1 shows their enrolments.

FIG. 8.1

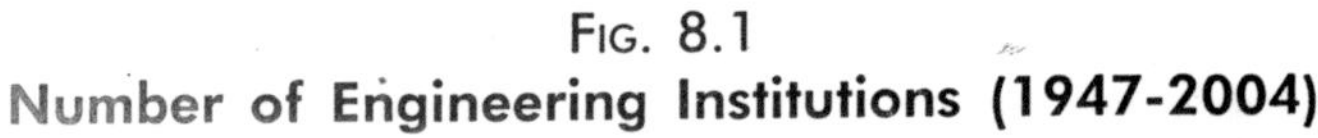

Number of Engineering Institutions (1947-2004)

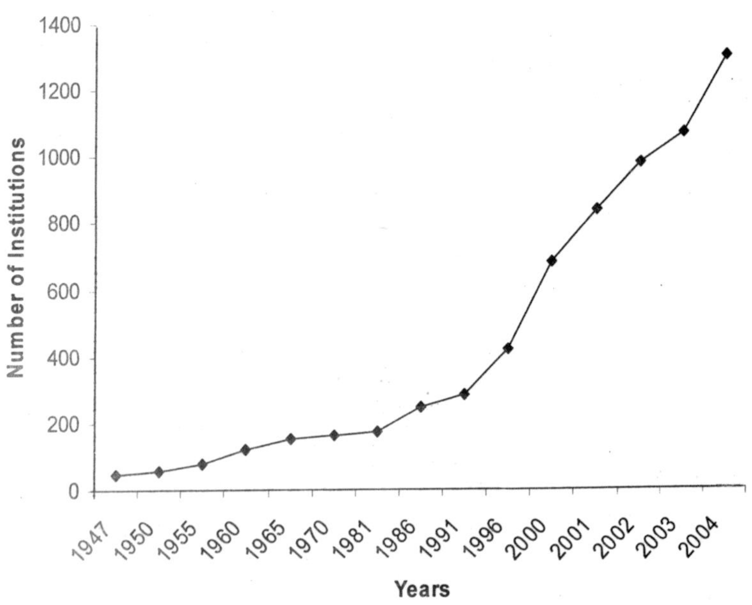

As seen in Figure 8.1, a large number of engineering institutions have come up since Independence. The number has reached 1,304 in the year 2004 from 46 in 1947. On the other hand, the growth of enrolment is not impressive. (Table 8.1) When we analyze the enrolment data in relative terms, the result seems to be very negligible. Tables 8.2 and 8.3 show the share of engineering education to total higher education and the number of engineering graduates per one lakh population.

TABLE 8.1
Enrolments in Engineering Education in India (1970-71 to 2005-06)

Year	*Enrolment in Engineering Education*	*Year*	*Enrolment in Engineering Education*
1970-71	87257	1988-89	201289
1971-72	82804	1989-90	209371
1972-73	82674	1990-91	216837
1973-74	86665	1991-92	258028
1974-75	90685	1992-93	271213
1975-76	96067	1993-94	285045
1976-77	100040	1994-95	299583
1977-78	103706	1995-96	315720
1978-79	111659	1996-97	331017
1979-80	118607	1997-98	346833
1980-81	128937	1998-99	363481
1981-82	130189	1999-2000	389001
1982-83	142440	2000-01	529469
1983-84	153131	2001-02	605597
1984-85	159046	2002-03	692087
1985-86	176540	2003-04	716652
1986-87	183966	2004-05	754635
1987-88	192148	2005-06	795120

Source : UGC, *Annual Reports* (Various Years).

As shown in Table 8.2 the growth of engineering education to total higher education is slow over the years. In the early Seventies it has shown a declining trend and afterwards it is stagnant for a decade or so. The share has increased to 7 per cent in recent years. On the other hand, the number of engineering graduates per one lakh population is also in an alarming condition (Table 8.3). The figure was less than 20 up to the early Eighties and has increased to 71 only in 2005-06, whereas it is much higher in case of China and other developing

Table 8.2
Share of Engineering Education to Total Higher Education in India (1970-71 to 2005-06)

Year	*Enrolment in Higher Education*	*Enrolment in Engineering Education*	*% of Engineering Enrolment to Total Higher Education*
(1)	*(2)*	*(3)*	*(4)*
1970-71	1,953,700	87,257	4.5
1971-72	2,065,041	82,804	4.0
1972-73	2,168,107	82,674	3.8
1973-74	2,234,385	86,665	3.9
1974-75	2,366,541	90,685	3.8
1975-76	2,426,109	96,067	3.9
1976-77	2,431,563	100,040	4.1
1977-78	2,564,972	103,706	4.0
1978-79	2,618,228	111,659	4.3
1979-80	2,648,579	118,607	4.8
1980-81	2,752,437	128,937	4.7
1981-82	2,952,066	130,189	4.4
1982-83	3,133,093	142,440	4.5
1983-84	3,307,649	153,131	4.6
1984-85	3,404,096	159,046	4.7
1985-86	3,605,029	176,540	4.9
1986-87	3,757,158	183,966	4.9
1987-88	4,020,159	192,148	4.8
1988-89	4,285,489	201,289	4.7
1989-90	4,602,680	209,371	4.5
1990-91	4,924,868	216,837	4.4
1991-92	5,265,886	258,028	4.9
1992-93	5,534,966	271,213	4.9
1993-94	5,817,249	285,045	4.9
1994-95	6,113,929	299,583	4.9

(Contd.)

TABLE 8.2 (Contd.)

(1)	(2)	(3)	(4)
1995-96	6,574,005	315,720	4.8
1996-97	6,842,598	331,017	4.8
1997-98	7,260,418	346,833	4.8
1998-99	7,705,520	363,481	4.7
1999-2000	8,050,607	389,001	4.8
2000-01	8,399,443	529,469	6.3
2001-02	8,964,680	605,597	6.7
2002-03	9,516,773	692,087	7.2
2003-04	9,953,506	716,652	7.2
2004-05	10,481,042	754,635	7.2
2005-06	11,028,020	795,120	7.2

Source : UGC, *Annual Reports* (Various Years).

TABLE 8.3
Availability of Engineering Graduates per Lakh Population in India (1970-71 to 2005-06)

Year	*Engineering graduates per lakh Population*	*Year*	*Engineering graduates per lakh Population*
(1)	(2)	(3)	(4)
1970-71	16.1	1988-89	25.0
1971-72	14.9	1989-90	25.4
1972-73	14.5	1990-91	25.8
1973-74	14.9	1991-92	30.1
1974-75	15.2	1992-93	31.1
1975-76	15.8	1993-94	31.9
1976-77	16.1	1994-95	32.9
1977-78	16.3	1995-96	34.0
1978-79	17.2	1996-97	34.9
1979-80	17.8	1997-98	35.9

(Contd.)

TABLE 8.3 (Contd.)

(1)	(2)	(3)	(4)
1980-81	18.9	1998-99	36.9
1981-82	18.8	1999-2000	38.8
1982-83	20.1	2000-01	51.9
1983-84	21.1	2001-02	58.3
1984-85	21.5	2002-03	65.6
1985-86	23.3	2003-04	66.7
1986-87	23.8	2004-05	69.2
1987-88	24.3	2005-06	71.8

Source : UGC, *Annual Reports* (Various Years).

nations of the world. The figure is also less in comparison to other disciplines of the study.

On the one hand, we are showing a dismal picture in engineering education by estimating its share to higher education and the number of engineering students per lakh population (Tables 8.2 and 8.3), which on the other side there is a massive unemployment among engineers. It is creating a dilemma among policy-maker and educationists whether there is a need to expand engineering education in India or not. The quality of engineering education in India is also a subject of concern. This is discussed in the following section of the paper.

EMERGING ISSUES IN ENGINEERING EDUCATION IN INDIA

Engineering education in India faces a number of issues despite its quantitative expansion. The two major issues are the uneven access by various social groups and geographical regions and the quality aspect of engineering education. These issues are the major focus of this Section. Engineering and technical education in India has been highly selective in terms of providing social access to the disadvantaged sections of the society such as scheduled castes, scheduled tribes and women. The participation of SCs and STs is less than 5 per cent at undergraduate level of education (Rao, 2006). The participation of students from low socio-economic strata is very low in technical institutions. About 82 per cent of the students in the IITs come from urban areas with a high level of income and a similar kind of trend is also noticed in case of NITs. Again, the number of technical institutions has also exploded in geographic pockets. The noted institutions like IITs, NITs are still a far reaching fact for most of the rural people. The four southern states (Andhra Pradesh, Kerala, Karnataka, and Tamil Nadu) and Maharashtra combined together constitute almost 60 per cent of the country's engineering institutions whereas the eastern and northern states are having only 16 per cent. In terms of undergraduate enrolment, the divide is even more prominent. Nationally, an average of 350 students per million people enter technical degree programmes, in the south the figure is 1,047, South-west, 689, West 486, East 131 and in the North it is only 102. The lack of regulation and planning by the AICTE has allowed for oversupply and undersupply in technical manpower in different regions of the country (WENR, 2007).

The share of women in engineering education is insignificant. This is also an important issue of concern for the policy-makers. There is a huge gap between boys' enrolment and the enrolment of girls in engineering education in India. Table 8.4 presents this. In 1980-81, the share of women to total enrolment was around 4 per cent and over a span of 26 years it has increased to 23 per cent. The growth is not satisfactory over the years and the issue needs serious attention.

Even though India is the second largest producer of engineering graduates in the world after China, the quality of engineering education is a great question mark because of the unplanned and uneven growth of this discipline. Data show that the expansion in the number of institutions of engineering and technical education apparently has taken place not in the state sector but in the private sector. After the Nineties there was massive expansion of private self-financed colleges and simultaneously the withdrawal of the state from further expansion of engineering and technical institutes. This led to the decline of quality. This is due to the fact that a large number of

TABLE 8.4
Participation of Women in Engineering Education (1980-81 to 2005-06)

Year	*Women Enrolment in Engineering Education*	*% of Women Enrolment in Engineering Education*
1980-81	4,949	3.8
1981-82	5,866	4.5
1982-83	7,173	5.0
1983-84	8,469	5.5
1984-85	10,052	6.3
1985-86	12,182	6.9
1986-87	12,694	6.9
1987-88	13,555	7.0
1988-89	14,591	7.2
1989-90	15,840	7.5
1990-91	17,130	7.8
1991-92	18,430	7.1
1992-93	19,840	7.3
1993-94	20,026	7.0
1994-95	24,850	8.2
1995-96	26,368	8.3
1996-97	27,638	8.3
1997-98	51,360	14.8
1998-99	54,055	14.8
1999-2000	63,057	16.2
2000-01	1,09,069	20.5
2001-02	1,31,792	21.7
2002-03	1,54,041	22.2
2003-04	1,65,316	23.0
2004-05	1,75,725	23.2
2005-06	1,85,800	23.3

Source : UGC, *Annual Reports* (Various years).

these self-financed colleges lack infrastructure, teaching staff, sometimes even basic equipment for laboratory work. Even in case of the state sector, reduced funding for technical education has hindered quality improvement.

The lack of adequate and qualified number of faculty in engineering education in India is also an important factor for low quality (Varshney, 2006). If we analyze the data of annual production of Ph.Ds, then it is very negligible and much less than required. According to a study cited in the Rao Report, an additional 10,000 doctorates were needed by 2008 to adequately staff engineering institutions across the country, whereas the latest data show that India was able to produce only 968 Ph.Ds in 2005-06 (Figure 8.2). The number of engineering doctorates awarded each year is less than one per cent of the total engineering graduates awarded every year. However, international comparison shows that, in most of the countries like China and USA, the number of Ph.D. degrees awarded annually range between 5-9 per cent of the engineering graduate degrees awarded. Involvement of industry to sponsor special doctoral fellowships was one of the ways to attract good students to the Ph.D. programme. Besides, improving the Ph.D. experience and facilitating challenging careers after Ph.D. could also increase the number of Ph.Ds (Banerjee, 2007). The Figure 8.2 shows the trend in the award of engineering doctorates in India.

Another important aspect of engineering and technical education in India is the poor linkage between the institutions and the industry. The industry and engineering institutions are closely connected through a symbiotic relationship. Technical institutions are engaged in educating engineers and the industry employs them on completion of their education. There is heavy interdependency between technical education and industry. Hence, there is a need for strategic policy interventions and industry-government-academia interaction in order to strengthen engineering education in the country. There is need for greater interaction between industry and the education system so that institutions of higher education can better understand the manpower needs of the market place and tailor their academic programs accordingly, especially as relates to the

Fig. 8.2
Ph.Ds Awarded in Engineering Education in India (1973-74 to 2004-05)

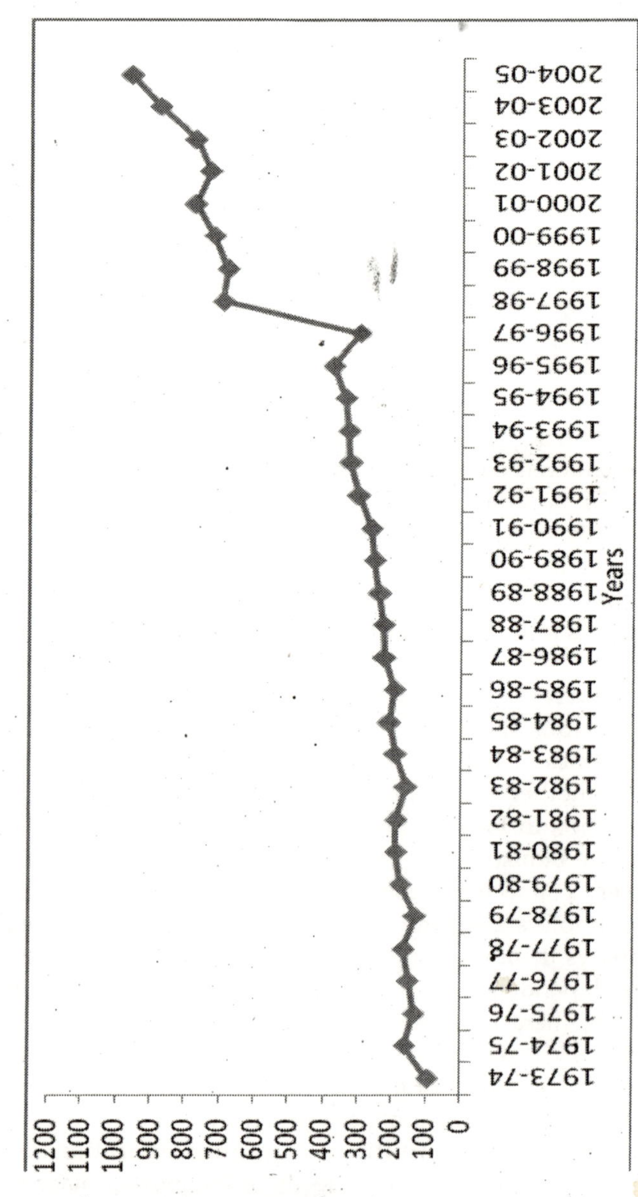

service sector and information technology (Banerjee, 2007). The industries should provide soft loans to the needy students for their academic improvement and the policy-making bodies should facilitate this process. Consequently, the whole system will work like a tri-polar process and the three poles are the institutions, government and industries.

TESTING FOR STRUCTURAL STABILITY BETWEEN PCI AND THE ENROLMENT IN ENGINEERING EDUCATION (CHOW TEST)

The structural change means that the values of the parameters of the model may not remain same during the entire study period. In 1991 the new economic policies have brought significant changes in the Indian higher education sector in general and engineering and technical education in particular. This may result in a structural change in the demand for engineering education before and after 1991. To test this, Chow test has been applied by considering the per capita income at constant prices as independent variable and the enrolment in engineering education as the dependant variable. For the given data, the Ordinary Least Squares (OLS) regression of per capita income on enrolment in engineering education for three periods namely pre-liberalization (1970-71 to 1990-91), post-liberalization (1991-92 to 2004-05) and the total study period (1970-71 to 2004-05) has been employed. The regression equations for these three periods are as follows:

Pre-liberalization period (1970-71 to 1990-91):

$$Y_t = \lambda_1 + \lambda_2 X_t + \eta_{1t} \quad \ldots\ldots (1)$$

Post-liberalization period (1991-92 to 2004-05):

$$Y_t = \gamma_1 + \gamma_2 X_t + \eta_{2t} \quad \ldots\ldots (2)$$

Total study period (1970-71 to 2004-05)

$$Y_t = \alpha_1 + \alpha_2 X_t + \eta_t \quad \ldots\ldots (3)$$

Where,

X_t = Per capita net national product (at 1999-2000 prices),
Y_t = Enrolment in engineering education,
η_{1t} = Error term for pre-liberalization period,
η_{2t} = Error term for post-liberalization period, and
η_t = Error term for total study period.

For all the above mentioned equations, the autocorrelation of the error terms are tested by means of DW statistic. However, it is assumed that the variances of all the error terms are equal (homoskedastic).

Equations 1 and 2 assume that the intercept and regression coefficients in the pre- and post-liberalization period are different.

The estimated values of the above said equations are obtained through Ordinary Least Square (OLS) and the data on variables are in logarithmic forms.

Pre-liberalization period (1970-71 to 1990-91):

$$\ln \hat{Y}_t = 10.08 + 2.39 \ln X_t \qquad \ldots\ldots (4)$$

(6.69) (14.49)

$R^2 = 0.91$, $RSS_1 = 0.18$,
df = 19, DW Statistic = 2.05

Post- liberalization period (1991-92 to 2004-05):

$$\ln \hat{Y}_t = 6.74 + 2.03 \ln X_t \qquad \ldots\ldots (5)$$

(4.08) (11.94)

$R^2 = 0.91$, $RSS_2 = 0.19$,
df = 13, DW Statistic = 2.08

Total study period (1970-71 to 2004-05):

$$\ln \hat{Y}_t = 7.82 + 2.15 \ln X_t \qquad \ldots\ldots (6)$$

(14.49) (37.25)

$R^2 = 0.976$, $RSS_3 = 0.41$,
df = 34, DW Statistic = 1.95

Where,

df represents the degrees of freedom,

RSS represents the residual sum of squares and the figures in the parentheses indicate the estimated t-values.

From the above estimated regressions, it is evident that the relationship between per capita income and the enrolment in engineering education are not same in the pre- and post-liberalization periods.

In the pre-liberalization period (1970-71 to 1990-91), the regression coefficient indicates that 1 per cent increase in per capita income leads to 2.39 per cent increase in enrolment where as in the post-liberalization period (1991-92 to 2004-05) the regression coefficient reveals that 1 per cent increase in per capita income leads to 2.03 per cent increase in enrolment. However, this small decline in the regression coefficient from pre-liberalization period to post-liberalization period may be attributed to the liberalized economic and educational policies adopted by the Government of India and to the external factors.

The pooled regression (Equation 3) includes all 36 observations of the study period and runs a common regression; disregarding possible differences in the sub-periods may not be appropriate. From the estimated equation it is evident that 1 per cent increase in industrial sector's contribution leads to 2.15 per cent increase in enrolment in engineering education. Hence, the coefficient of income elasticity for engineering education is 2.15 which is elastic in nature. The reasons may be attributed to the high course fee of higher engineering and technical education.

These results need to be supported by appropriate statistical tests. The structural changes may cause the differences in the intercept or the coefficient or both; hence it is tested with the help of Chow test and for this we need to compare between computed and critical F value. If the computed value exceeds the critical one we reject the null hypothesis and conclude that there is the structural change, otherwise we do not reject the null hypothesis and hence there is no structural change.

In the present analysis, the computed F-value (1.81) is smaller than the critical F-value (5.28) at 1 percent level of significance and hence the null hypothesis is not rejected. It means that the relation between the per capita income and the enrolment in engineering education has not undergone a structural change in India during the period from 1970-71 to 2004-05.

CONCLUSION

It is now well-recognized that engineering and technical education is a catalyst for the growth and development of a developing country like India. It is, therefore, imperative for the nation to develop a well-integrated technical education system to keep pace with the changing world. It needs to address a few challenges faced by our higher engineering education sector and accordingly steps should be undertaken. First, to maintain quality and to reduce the unemployment and under-employment level, the right kind of engineering and technical education should be imparted and the policy should be redesigned accordingly. In the present competitive world, the country needs only the right kind of education, which is possible with the help of strong manpower planning. For the enhancement of quality, adequate and qualified faculty should be appointed and steps should be taken to retain them in the academic sphere. There should be control over the opening and recognizing of engineering education by private agencies. These institutions are interested in making engineering and technical education as a profit-making venture or business. Here, the AICTE plays an important role to control their activities and it should take utmost care for this issue. Secondly, there is a huge disparity that exists among geographic regions with regard to participation in engineering education. It is highly uneven. The concentration of the facilities in certain parts of the country, leaving out some others has brought out the deficiencies in the national level planning and coordination (Rao, 2006). There is, therefore, a need to open institutions in unserved regions by the state. Finally, the issue of unequal access of different social groups such as women and other disadvantaged groups like scheduled castes and scheduled tribes should be taken care of both by the state and the private sector. The exclusion of these groups are creating imbalance in the growth and development of engineering and technical education in the country.

After discussing all the above issues it is clear that technical education is a basic and essential input for national development and for strengthening our industry, economy and the quality of life of the people. This aspect has been reflected in the Eleventh Five-Year Plan document which envisages major expansion in the number of centrally-funded technical education institutions by proposing to set-up 8 new IITs, 7 more IIMs, 20 new IIITs within the Plan period. The outcome is to be seen in the days to come.

REFERENCES

Agarwal, Pawan (2005) "Engineering Education in India: Changing Global Realities and Responses", *University News*, Vol. 43, No. 39, pp. 35-41.

Banerjee, R. and Muley, V.P. (2007) 'Engineering Education in India', Draft Final Report, Observer Research Foundation, Mumbai, IIT Bombay.

Banerjee, S. and Bandopadhyay, S. (2004) "Technical Education in India: Need of the Hour", *Margin*, Vol. 36, No. 2, pp. 61-68.

Bhunia, C.T. (2003) "Technical Education: Some Thoughts", *University News*, Vol. 41, No. 02, pp. 1-4.

Fuller, C.J. and Narasimhan, H. (2006) "Engineering Colleges, 'Exposure' and Information Technology: Professionals in Tamil Nadu", *Economic Political Weekly*, January 21, pp. 258-62.

Gereffi and *et. al.* (2008) "Getting the Numbers Right: International Engineering Education in the United States, China and India", *Journal of Engineering Education*, Vol. 97, No. 1, pp. 13-25.

Government of India, *Economic Survey of India, 2007-08*, New Delhi, Oxford University Press.

Government of India, Ministry of Human Resources Development, *Selected Educational Statistics*, 2004-05, New Delhi, MHRD.

Government of India, Ministry of Education and Culture. (1980) *Report of the Review Committee on Post-Graduate Education and Research in Engineering and Technology*, New Delhi, Ministry of Education and Culture.

Gujarati, D.N. (2004) *Basic Econometrics*, New Delhi, Tata McGraw-Hill.

Jha, C.S. (2005) "Global Issues in Engineering Education", *University News*, Vol. 43, No. 39, pp. 13-29.

IAMR (2007) *Manpower Profile*, India Year Book, New Delhi, IAMR.

Rao, S.S. (2006) "Engineering and Technology Education in India: Uneven Spread, Quality and Social Coverage", *Journal of Educational Planning and Administration*, Vol. 20, No. 2, pp. 205-25.

Shah, Beena and Mishra, P.K. (1996) "Technical Education: Historical Review and Future Prospects", *University News*, Vol. 34, No. 50, pp. 1-5.

Sharan, R. (2004) "Engineering Education in India: A Critical Look", *IASSI Quarterly*, Vol. 23, No. 1, pp. 63-79.

Sharma, P.B. (2005) "Engineering Profession at Crossroads", *University News*, Vol. 43, No. 39, pp. 79-82.

Tilak, J.B.G. (1995) "Higher Education at Cross-roads", *Journal of Higher Education*, Vol. 18, No. 4, pp. 595-605.

University Grants Commission (UGC). *Annual Reports* (Various years), New Delhi, UGC.

Varshney, L.R. (2006) 'Private Engineering Education in India: Market Failures and Regulatory Solutions', Unpublished Writing, No. 4, Massachusetts Institute of Technology, USA.

World Education News and Reviews (2007), 'Engineering Education in India: A Story of Contrasts', January. http://www.wes.org/ewenr/07jan/feature.htm (Last accessed on August 25, 2008).

9

Higher Education and Growth of the Indian Economy : The Emerging Scenario in Relation to Inter-State Disparities

MANISH DEV

India with 2.4 per cent of the world surface area and a whopping 16.7 per cent of the world population is the fourth largest economy of the world in terms of PPP (purchasing power parity) after the USA, China and Japan. The one billion plus population is residing in 28 States and 7 Union Territories under a quasi federal structure. There are wide variations across these states/UTs in regard to physical geography, culture, manpower and other socio-economic conditions. The Indian economy has crossed over the regime of 'Hindu Growth Rate' (2.5% to 3.5%) and secured a path of 'Secured Growth Rate' (5-6%). At present, it is the second fastest growing economy of the world after China. But this growth scenario is uneven in the sense that some states have achieved rapid economic growth of the order of 10 per cent or more, while others have languished.

For an economy growing at 9 per cent plus per annum, the need for a skilled work force increases immeasurably and enough concern has been voiced by industry and global analysis that if there is one field in which India has to do some rapid catching up, it is education in general and higher education in particular. But the need for higher education enhancement opportunities is not simply rooted in the contingent needs of the economy. It is also a way to make growth more inclusive and more evenly distributed. Despite six decades of planning and existence of world-class institutions of higher learning, a large section of the population does not have access to basic education, what to say of higher education. According to a report of the Ministry of Human Resource Development, out of a total of 19.4 crore children in the 6-13 age group, 1.34 crore (6.94 per cent) were out of school in July-October 2005 (Bhagat, 2007). More shockingly, the survey estimated that out of those children not in school, 68.3 per cent have never been to school and 31.7 per cent are drop-outs after one or more years of schooling. The situation is worse at higher education level. As the young Indians move up the education chain, a large number of youths never make it to the college or university level. The Gross Enrolment Ratio for class 9-12 in 2004-05 was 39.91 per cent; note the drop in the ratio from 51.65 per cent for class 9 and 10 to only 27.82 per cent for classes 11 to 12. While only 27 per cent of children in India do not reach up to higher secondary education level (Class 11 and 12), those reaching college and universities constitute a smaller percentage (Bhagat, 2007). The access and quality of higher education in India is not up to the mark as per the requirement of a rapidly growing economy. India faces the biggest challenge of finding adequately skilled, educated and trained manpower because of its GDP growth rate. India's current GDP is $ 1.25 trillion and at an annual growth rate of 7 per cent, it could double to $ 2.5 trillion in 10 years. But what could derail our growth is finding skilled and trained manpower (Pai, 2008).

The objective of this paper is to try to make some sense of the differential performance of Indian higher education system in relation to economic growth in the recent past. The paper is divided into four sections. The First section deals with the growth pattern of Indian states during the last decades of planning. The Second section covers the growth of Indian higher education system in terms of access and equity. The Third section concentrates on the quality aspects of higher education and finally, the Fourth section is a concluding one.

GROWTH PATTERN OF INDIAN ECONOMY DURING PLANS

The Indian economy has grown steadily over all the Five-Year Plans (Table 9.1). It is another thing that growth performances were varied in different plans. Percentage growth rates of GDP were well short of the targeted growth rates from Second to Fourth Five Year Plan. From the Fifth Plan to Eighth Plan, growth rates achieved were consistently higher than those targeted. The trend has broken with a shortfall in the targeted growth in the Ninth and Tenth Plans. However, the economy has moved decisively to a higher growth phase, with growth rate at market prices exceeding 8 per cent in every year since 2003-04. The GDP growth rate during 2005-06 and 2006-07 was

TABLE 9.1
Growth Rates of GDP of the Indian Economy

Plan	*GDP Growth Rate (%)*
First Five-Year Plan	3.6
Second Five-Year Plan	4.3
Third Five-Year Plan	2.8
Fourth Five-Year Plan	3.3
Fifth Five-Year Plan	4.8
Sixth Five-Year Plan	5.7
Seventh Five-Year Plan	6.0
Eighth Five-Year Plan	6.8
Ninth Five-Year Plan	5.3
Tenth Five-Year Plan	7.9

Source : Government of India, *Draft Eleventh Five-Year Plan*, Vol. I.

Table 9.2

State-wise Growth Rates of NSDP and per capita NSDP at Current Prices, Literacy Rates, GER in Higher Education and Ratio of Graduate and Above in Total Literate

State	*NSDP growth rate 1999-2006*	*Per capita NSDP growth rate 1999-2006*	*Literacy rate 2001*	*GER (%) in higher education SES (2000)*	*Ratio of graduate and above (%) (2001)*
(1)	(2)	(3)	(4)	(5)	(6)
Andhra Pradesh	10.07	8.87	60.5	9.66	7.08
Assam	9.19	7.29	63.3	9.40	4.84
Bihar	7.09	4.95	47.0	6.16	6.78
Gujarat	13.41	11.43	69.1	10.01	6.29
Haryana	12.25	9.90	67.9	9.99	6.60
Himachal Pradesh	10.09	8.25	76.5	15.22	5.46
Jammu & Kashmir	9.24	6.55	56.5	9.78	6.90
Karnataka	9.82	8.40	66.6	7.96	7.32
Kerala	9.53	8.40	90.9	18.08	5.66
Maharashtra	10.36	8.58	76.9	14.14	7.64
Madhya Pradesh	6.53	4.48	63.7	10.48	6.11
Orissa	11.02	9.81	63.1	8.21	5.97

Punjab	6.74	4.90	69.7	10.86	6.51
Rajasthan	7.92	5.64	60.4	8.85	5.31
Tamil Nadu	8.22	7.28	73.5	12.05	5.42
Uttar Pradesh	8.12	5.95	56.3	9.59	6.56
West Bengal	9.40	8.06	68.6	6.30	6.75
All India	10.17	8.40	64.8	10.08	6.70

Notes : (i) For NSDP growth rate and per capita NSDP growth rate; *Economic Survey, 2007-08.*
(ii) For literacy rate; *Economic Survey 2007-08.*
(iii) For GER; *Inter-Ministry Task Group of Planning Commission.*
(iv) For ratio of Graduate and above; *Census of India, 2001.*

9.2 per cent that made the Indian economy the second fastest growing economy of the world after China. However, the growth pattern of the country is not evenly distributed as is reflected in Table 9.2.

There are wide variations in growth performance among the states. Punjab, Haryana and Himachal Pradesh were the top performers during the Sixties and were well ahead of the national average, while all the BIMARU states along with Andhra Pradesh could register growth rate of 0.7-1.6 per cent. Punjab and Haryana maintained their top slot even during the Seventies while Maharashtra remained at the top. None of the BIMARU states could improve their position and remained well below the national average. The situation changed considerably during the Eighties when Rajasthan, a BIMARU state emerged as the front runner with 5.9 per cent growth rate and attained third position. Haryana was at the top while Punjab slipped to sixth place. The poorer states like Orissa, Uttar Pradesh, Bihar and Madhya Pradesh improved their position too. The era of economic reform witnessed an improvement in the performance of the states having a sound manufacturing base. Therefore, states like Karnataka, Gujarat, Tamil Nadu, Rajasthan, Maharashtra and West Bengal attained higher position in the growth ladder. During 1990-2000 to 2005-06 the exponential growth rate of NSDP at current prices is as high as 13.41 per cent for Gujarat which is at the top. Haryana again emerged as a fast moving state occupying the second position. Notably, Orissa which is a poor performer so far has registered a growth rate of 11.02 per cent and reached the third position. So is the case with Andhra Pradesh that moved to higher place for the first time. The BIMARU states remained well below the national average during the first half of the new millennium.

Thus, it is clear from the above discussion that discrepancies between income growth of states have widened, with richer states having grown faster than the poorer states. There are differences in incomes within states, such as between rural and urban areas, between gender and in individual incomes (Agarwal, 2008). The Inter-Ministry Task Group on Redressing Growing Regional Imbalances identified 170 most backward districts including 55 extremely affected districts in the country. Even in highly developed states, there are regions and districts whose indicators are comparable to those of the poorest districts in the most backward states. Despite the efforts made, regional disparities have continued to grow and the gaps have been accentuated as the benefits of economic growth have been largely continued to concentrate in better developed areas (GoI, 2007).

These disparities are also reflected in the attainment of education. Data regarding literacy rate reveal that all the highly developed states have higher literacy rates (Kerala with a moderate growth rate is an exception to this). The World Bank Development Policy Review finds high correlation between literacy rate and rank in GDP per capita. Four lowest ranked states in terms of GDP per capita also ranked lowest in HDI, with Bihar, Uttar Pradesh and Rajasthan ranking lowest in literacy rates as well (Agarwal, 2008). The Standard Deviation of 1.85 in relation to growth rate of NSDP at current price, 1.96 in relation to growth rate of per capita NSDP at current prices confirm that there are disparities among states in the growth pattern. This disparity is more significant in literacy rate and Gross Enrolment Ratio in higher education. However, data regarding the ratio of graduate and above to total literate people in the states shows more consistency (Tables 9.2 and 9.3).

Coefficient of correlation between growth rate of per capita NSDP at current prices and literacy rate is +0.405, which confirms that states with higher per capita income have higher literacy rate. A lower correlation coefficient between per capita income growth and ratio of graduate and above to total literate population shows that high growth rate of per capita income does not necessarily result in attainment of a degree. Highly literate Kerala has only 5.66 per cent graduates and above out of the total literate persons in the state. On the contrary, a poorer state Bihar has 6.78 per cent graduate and more persons out of the total literate population which is above the national average. It is also noteworthy that Bihar has lowest gross enrolment ratio in the country, but has more graduate ratio. And Kerala with highest Gross Enrolment Ratio has a very low level of graduate and above ratio. So is the case with Himachal Pradesh and Tamil Nadu. Maharashtra is the only state in the list with a high GER and high ratio of graduate and above population to total literate population. The above phenomenon has the following explanations:

1. Younger generation in Bihar (along with Jharkhand prefer civil services and thus acquiring a degree is a pre-condition to that.
2. Younger generation in Kerala and Tamil Nadu prefer job-oriented courses after senior secondary education and for them graduation is not a necessity.
3. Younger generation in Andhra Pradesh, Karnataka and Maharashtra prefer the degree level education, especially in engineering and technology because of easy availability of engineering and technological institutions in these states.

GROWTH OF HIGHER EDUCATION IN INDIA

In its size and diversity, India has the third largest higher education system in the world, next only to China and USA. Access to higher education was very limited before independence, with enrolment of less than a million students in 500 colleges and 20 universities. The growth of higher education, at least quantitatively, appears to be very impressive since independence as the number of universities has increased from 20 in 1947-48 to 367 in 2006 (18 times) and the number of colleges from 496 in 1947-48 to 18064 in 2005-06 (35 times) and enrolment from 0.2 million in 1947-48 to 13.93 million in 2005-06 (69 times) (GOI, 2006-07).

The Indian higher education system is now more mass-based and democratized with one-third to 40 per cent of students coming from lower socio-economic status and women comprising about 35 per cent of the enrolments (Tilak, 2006). In the sphere of technical education by 2004 India had 1478 engineering and technical colleges, 629 pharmacy colleges, 118 architecture, 71 hotel management and 5190 teacher education colleges making a total of about 7486 institutions. In respect of post-graduate educational institutions there are 1052 MBA/PGDBM and 97 MCA colleges in 2005-06.

TABLE 9.3
Growth of Higher Education Institutions and Enrolment in India

Year	*Universities*	*Colleges*	*Total HEIs*	*Enrolment (in millions)*
1947-48	20	496	516	0.2
1950-51	30	578	608	0.2
1960-61	45	1,819	1,864	0.6
1970-71	93	3,277	3,370	2.0
1980-81	123	4,738	4,861	2.8
1990-91	184	5,748	5,932	4.4
2000-01	266	11,146	11,412	8.8
2005-06	367	18,064	21,431	13.9

Note : Universities include Central, state, private and deemed-to-be universities and institutions of national importance established by the Central and state governments.

Source : UGC documents.

In terms of distribution, there are some distinguishing features in the distribution of colleges in different states. There is a north-south imbalance in the number of colleges. Southern states such as Maharashtra, Andhra Pradesh and Karnataka have 2441, 2096 and 1865 colleges respectively, which together constitute 36 per cent of the total colleges in the country. Some of the major northern states such as Assam, Bihar, Uttaranchal, West Bengal, and Jharkhand lag behind other states with regard to the number of colleges. Even the larger northern states, such as Uttar Pradesh, Madhya Pradesh and Rajasthan have less number of colleges as compared to their southern counterparts.

GROWTH IN STUDENT ENROLMENT

Growth of higher education is best judged by analyzing two key factors: (i) Gross enrolment ratio at higher education level, i.e. access, and (ii) Quality of higher education. Another factor that gives a better picture of the growth of higher education is a comparison of its demand and supply aspects. In its supply side what need to be ascertained is that all those who have passed senior secondary examination are eligible and willing to join higher education must have an access to an institution of higher learning. Secondly, the growth of higher education, both in terms of number and diversification, must meet the growing manpower needs of the economy in terms of supplying skilled manpower to the economy. Although the number of colleges in almost every discipline have increased significantly during the Ninth and Tenth Five-Year Plan periods, these are not adequate to accommodate all those students who pass their intermediate examinations.

Gross Enrolment Ratio (GER) is a good measure to assess the access to education in the country/region/class. It is the ratio of students enrolled at each level of education, as a proportion of the population of the relevant age group. In case of higher education the relevant age group is 18-24 years. GER in India was only 11 per cent in 2001, which was the lowest among the selected countries presented in Table 9.4. It was as high as 81 per cent in USA, 70 per cent in Russia, 64 per cent in UK and 54 per cent in France. The GER was higher in the fast developing countries such as Brazil, Indonesia, Malaysia and China (Table 9.4).

The total enrolment in higher education is presented in Table 9.8 which reveals that 11.2 million students were enrolled in different disciplines in the country in 2003-04. The total enrolment in Ph.D. and Post-graduate courses is 65,525 and 8,06,636 respectively, which shows a rather low research base in relation to total enrolment in higher education. Technical education has grown at 364.26 per cent as compared to 325.46 per cent during the period 1980-81 to 2003-04.

There are some notable changes in enrolment pattern in India during the last 25 years. The graduate enrolment as a proportion to total enrolment is increasing, the post-graduate enrolment as a proportion to total enrolment is almost constant at 8 per cent. Science and technology graduate as a proportion to total graduate has declined from 32 per cent in 1980 to 29 per cent in 2003. The recent years have also witnessed a decline in the number of science graduates in relation to technical graduates. Despite this the ratio of technical to total graduates remains as low as 8 per cent. As the demand for teachers is on

TABLE 9.4

Growth in Higher Education (in Selected Countries)

Country	*Enrolment (in millions)*		*Percentage Increase*	*GER (%) 2001*	*GNP per capita (US $) 2004*
	1990-91	*2001-02*			
USA	13.71	15.93	16.2	81	34,280
China	3.82	12.14	217.7	13	890
India	4.95	10.58	113.6	11	460
Japan	2.90	3.97	36.8	49	35,610
UK	1.26	2.24	78.1	64	25,120
France	1.70	2.03	19.4	54	22,730
Italy	1.45	1.85	27.7	53	19,390
Brazil	1.54	3.113	103.0	18	,3070
Russia	5.10	9.02	57.3	70	1750
Canada	0.84	1.19	41.7	58	21,980
Indonesia	1.59	3.18	99.7	15	690
Philippines	1.71	2.47	44.3	31	1030
Australia	0.49	0.87	79.1	65	19,900
Malaysia	0.12	0.56	358.9	27	3,330

Sources : (i) For 1990-91—UNESCO, *Statistical Year Book.*
(ii) For 2001-02—UNESCO, Institute of statistics (2005).
(iii) For GNP per capita—UNESCO, EFA *Global Monitoring Reports* (2004).

the rise, the enrolment in B.Ed. courses is increasing, especially in northern states such as Uttar Pradesh, Uttaranchal, Madhya Pradesh, Rajasthan and Haryana. The fall in vocational enrolment to total enrolment in higher education is a matter of concern for higher education planners.

ENROLMENT AT DISAGGREGATE LEVEL

The following Section provides an analysis about the disparity in enrolment between: (i) rural and urban, (ii) interstate, (iii) inter-caste, (iv) Inter-religion, (v) based gender, (vi) occupation-wise, and (vii) poor and non-poor.

Table 9.5
Enrolment of Levels and Major Disciplines in India

Year	*Ph.D.*	*P.G.*	*General Graduate (Arts, Science and Commerce)*	*Technical Graduate (Engg., Medical, B.Ed.)*	*Total higher education (degree) (2+3+4+5)*	*Diploma*	*Total higher education (degree, diploma) (6+7)*
(1)	(2)	(3)	(4)	(5)	(6)	(7)	(8)
1980-81	25,417	291,341	1,886,428	239,267	2,442,453	430,126	2,872,579
1990-91	32,468	354,216	3,285,776	416,828	4,089,288	796,686	4,885,974
2000-01	45,004	647,338	7,244,915	688,625	8,625,882	987,279	9,613,161
2001-02	53,119	647,016	7,139,497	790,050	8,629,682	1,104,594	9,734,276
2002-03	65,357	782,590	7,633,125	1,035,701	9,516,773	1,199,785	10,716,558
2003-04	65,525	806,636	8,026,147	1,110,840	10,009,148	1,191,447	11,200,595

Source : Government of India, Ministry of Human Resource Development, *Selected Educational Statistics* (various years).

1. Rural and Urban

Significant disparities exist in GER between the rural and urban areas. GER for rural and urban areas was 7.76 per cent and 27.20 per cent respectively in 2003-04. It shows that the GER in urban areas is about four times high as compared to rural areas. The Eligible Enrolment Ratio worked out to be 51.1 per cent for rural areas and 66 per cent for urban areas—the later being higher by 15 percentage points. In simple terms it shows that only half of the rural students who pass their higher secondary examination go to higher education which is less by 15 percentage points compared to urban areas.

TABLE 9.6
Gross Enrolment Ratio in Rural and Urban Area in India (%)

	SES data 2003-04	*NSS data 99-2000*	*Census data 2001*
Rural area	7.76	5.58	8.99
Urban area	27.20	21.74	24.52

2. Inter-state Disparities in GER in Higher Education

There are considerable inter-state disparities in the level of higher education. According to NSS data the GER at aggregate level is about 10.08 per cent in 2000. It is more than the national average in states/UTs like Chandigarh (26.24%), Delhi (21.16%), Kerala (18.08%), Goa (17.56%), Pondicherry (15.37%), Himachal Pradesh (15.22%), and Maharashtra (14.15%). The GER is as low as 0.34 per cent in Lakshadweep, 2.23 per cent in Dadra and Nagar Haveli, 2.42 per cent in Arunachal Pradesh. A developed state like Karnataka has GER of only 7.96 per cent. West Bengal with a GER of 6.30 per cent produces only 14,000 engineers in a year.

3. Gender Disparities

The access to higher education is also low for girls as compared to boys. The GER for males is 12.12 per cent and 8 per cent for female. In case of SC females, it is only 3.48 per cent as compared to 14.11 per cent for general category females. For

TABLE 9.7
Access to Higher Education in India

States	*Gross Enrolment Ratio* (GER %) in Age Group 18-23 years, 1999-2000***					
	Total Graduates			*Total Higher Education*		
	Male	*Female*	*Total*	*Male*	*Female*	*Total*
(1)	*(2)*	*(3)*	*(4)*	*(5)*	*(6)*	*(7)*
Andhra Pradesh	9.03	5.57	7.25	12.16	7.29	9.66
Arunachal Pradesh	3.98	0.41	2.22	4.29	0.51	2.42
Assam	9.37	7.11	8.28	10.81	7.88	9.40
Bihar	6.92	2.84	4.91	8.79	3.47	6.16
Goa	7.55	11.57	9.71	18.69	16.55	17.54
Gujarat	8.78	7.43	8.11	11.22	8.80	10.01
Haryana	8.55	6.81	7.73	11.14	8.69	9.99
Himachal Pradesh	11.78	11.41	11.58	16.85	13.84	15.22
Jammu & Kashmir	9.44	6.83	8.17	11.19	8.30	9.78
Karnataka	6.68	3.94	5.31	10.06	5.86	7.96
Kerala	12.46	15.54	14.05	15.56	20.43	18.08
Madhya Pradesh	9.28	8.94	9.12	11.00	9.91	10.48
Maharashtra	11.13	8.08	9.70	16.81	11.10	14.14
Manipur	11.00	9.06	10.05	14.59	12.53	13.58
Meghalaya	6.62	5.40	5.99	7.22	7.05	7.13
Mizoram	8.39	2.98	5.61	10.23	5.63	7.87
Nagaland	13.28	13.44	13.35	13.93	14.15	14.04
Orissa	9.20	4.29	6.71	11.55	4.94	8.21
Punjab	8.01	7.25	7.65	10.14	11.64	10.86
Rajasthan	8.93	5.62	7.36	10.99	6.48	8.85
Sikkim	4.98	1.31	3.25	7.39	2.36	5.01
Tamil Nadu	11.83	7.30	9.45	15.23	9.19	12.05
Tripura	7.16	3.08	5.24	7.85	3.84	5.97
Uttar Pradesh	9.83	5.10	7.58	12.60	6.29	9.59
West Bengal	6.45	2.97	4.68	8.69	3.98	6.30

(Contd.)

TABLE 9.7 (Contd.)

(1)	(2)		(3)	(4)		
A & N Islands	4.28	10.43	7.56	4.33	11.04	7.91
Chandigarh	17.96	23.90	20.18	23.26	31.23	26.24
Delhi	13.74	20.27	16.38	19.73	23.26	21.16
Lakshadweep	0.00	0.57	0.34	0.00	0.57	0.34
Pondicherry	15.67	7.90	11.81	18.81	11.90	15.37
India	9.22	6.30	7.79	12.13	7.94	10.08

Notes : * GER = Total graduates and diploma enrolled/population in the 18-23 age group.

** These include only those enrolled and have attained higher secondary and above education.

Source : NSS, 1999-2000.

rural SC female the GER in higher education is only 1.70 per cent. Urban SC females are in better position in this regard.

TABLE 9.8

Access to Higher Education by Caste Group—2000

Socio-Religious Group	*Gross Enrolment Ratio (GER %) in Age Group 18-23 years (1999-2000)*		
	Total Higher Education		
	Male	*Female*	*Total*
(1)	*(2)*	*(3)*	*(4)*
ST	7.19	5.71	6.43
SC	6.63	3.48	5.09
OBC	8.99	4.91	7.00
General	19.20	14.11	16.74
Total	12.12	8.00	10.10
Rural			
ST	5.74	4.53	5.10

(*Contd.*)

TABLE 9.8 (*Contd.*)

(1)	(2)	(3)	(4)
SC	5.07	1.70	3.40
OBC	5.88	2.27	4.10
General	11.79	6.19	9.01
Total	7.53	3.61	5.58
Urban			
ST	17.08	14.56	15.83
SC	12.19	10.75	11.53
OBC	17.82	12.96	15.51
General	30.50	27.87	29.28
Total	23.28	19.99	21.74

Source : NSS, 1999-2000, Position with 10.75 per cent GER.

4. Occupational Variations in GER in Higher Education

Significant variations can be seen from Table 9.9 in GER in higher education among various occupational groups. In rural areas the GER for agricultural labourers is only 1.41 per cent as compared to 18.55 per cent for others. In urban areas casual the labourers have GER of only 3.26 per cent as compared to 50.15 per cent for others.

5. Inter-caste Variations

In 2003-04, the GER was about 13.22 per cent at over all level. However, there are significant disparities across social groups. The GER for STs, SCs, OBCs and others (non-SC/ST/OBC) was 5 per cent, 7.51 per cent, 11.34 per cent, 24.8 per cent, 5.08 per cent, 7.00 per cent and 16.74 per cent respectively in 1999-2000. Thus the GER for others is 5 times higher than STs, 3 times higher than SCs and about 2 times higher than OBCs in 2003-04.

6. Inter-religion Disparities

It is evident from Table 9.10 that the SC/ST/OBC people belonging to Hindu religion lag far behind the higher caste

Table 9.9
GER in Higher Education in India (1999-2000) per Occupational Structures of Household

HIH Type	*ST*	*SC*	*OBC*	*Others*	*All*
Rural					
Self-employment in non-agriculture	2.53	3.77	3.97	7.73	5.17
Agricultural labour	0.67	1.63	1.16	1.93	1.41
Other labour	0.91	1.52	4.26	4.02	2.99
Self-employed in agriculture	3.04	3.95	4.21	8.33	5.64
Others	35.39	14.15	11.54	22.08	18.55
All	5.12	3.38	4.10	9.00	5.58
Urban					
Self employed	6.15	7.37	10.05	22.09	15.74
Regular wage and salary	27.33	18.04	22.19	33.72	28.10
Casual labour	1.53	2.61	3.34	4.30	3.26
Others	40.38	29.52	41.57	59.60	50.15
All	15.87	11.55	15.53	29.28	21.75

Source : NSS, 1999-2000.

Table 9.10
Inter-state Disparities in GER in India

Year	*Source*	*Gross Enrolment Ratio in Higher Education*				
		ST	*SC*	*OBC*	*Others*	*Total*
1999-2000	NSS	6.43	5.08	7.00	16.74	10.10
2001	Census	7.46	8.39	9.29	15.57	13.80
2003-04	NSS	5.00	7.51	11.34	24.89	13.22

Hindu people. However, between various religious groups, the SCs from some religious groups suffer more in access to higher education than other for instance the GER of SC Buddhists is relatively high (14 per cent) followed by SC Christians (9.97 per cent), SC Hindu (4.88 per cent) and SC Sikh (2.33 per cent) (Thorat, 2006).

TABLE 9.11
GER on Religious Basis in India

(*in per cent*)

Religion	*NSS 2003*	*NSS 2000*				
		SC	*ST*	*OBC*	*Others*	*All*
Hindu	13.47	4.88	6.16	7.06	19.71	10.00
Muslim	8.19	1.83	4.14	3.94	5.91	5.30
Others	30.87	NA	NA	NA	NA	NA
Jain	57.43	NA	NA	NA	NA	NA
Christians	27.29	9.97	NA	NA	NA	NA
Sikhs/Buddhists	15.00	1.81	NA	NA	18.94	11.00
Total	13.22	6.43	5.08	7.00	16.74	10.10

7. Access to Higher Education for the Poor

It is seen from Table 9.11 that wide variation exists in access to higher education between the poor and non-poor according to NSS data for 1999-2000.

GER for the poor was 2.43 per cent which was almost six time lower compared with 12.81 per cent for non-poor. In rural and urban areas the GER for the poor was 1.30 per cent and 5.51 per cent for the non-poor respectively.

It can be concluded that growth of higher education is uneven with disparities with regard to its access to various sections of the society. The present status is not only inadequate, but also inefficient in the sense that it does not fulfill the aspirations of the weaker sections of the society. There are wide range of disparities which are prevalent on rural-urban, inter-state, inter-caste, inter-religion and gender basis. On regional basis states like Bihar, Jharkhand, Chhattisgarh, Orissa, West Bengal, Madhya Pradesh and all the North Eastern states lag far behind to their counterparts in the south. The SCs, STs and other backward castes and more particularly the females of these groups are worst placed in the field of higher education.

TABLE 9.12
Gross Enrolment Ratio for Poor and Non-poor in India : 1991-2000

Social Group	*Gross Enrolment Ratio*		
	Rural	*Urban*	*Total*
ST	1.11	4.78	1.55
SC	1.35	3.86	1.89
OBC	1.13	5.16	2.30
Others	1.66	7.00	3.58
All	1.30	5.51	2.43
	Non-Poor		
ST	7.81	23.19	9.7
SC	4.38	15.71	6.68
OBC	5.10	19.98	8.69
Others	10.74	34.01	19.73
All	7.12	27.15	12.81
	Entire Population		
ST	5.12	15.87	6.43
SC	3.38	11.55	5.08
OBC	4.10	15.53	7.00
Others	9.00	29.28	16.74
All	5.58	21.75	10.10

QUALITY AND EXCELLENCE IN HIGHER EDUCATION

Several recent studies have revealed that the Indian higher education system is facing a deepening crisis with declining standards and poor governance (Naik, 2006; Chauhan, 2006; Tilak, 2006; Thorat, 2006; Bharadwaj and Dev, 2007). Despite the existence of mechanism to maintain quality the overall standard of higher education has continued to deteriorate, thus reducing the value of an academic degree from most institutions of higher learning. According to sources in industry, only about a fourth of the graduates are employable. There is a growing shortage of skills alongside a high prevalence of unemployment among graduates (Naik, 2006).

The University Grants Commission came up with a startling admission that over half of the students who pass higher secondary education do not enter the higher education stream. About 90 per cent of the colleges and 68 per cent of the universities in India are of average or poor quality. The higher education system is in dire need of quality upgradation in almost all indicators of quality which includes faculty standard, library facilities, computer availability, teacher-student ratio, etc.

The quality gap in universities and colleges is alarming (NAAC, 2007).

- A quarter of faculty positions in the universities remain vacant.
- 57 per cent of the teachers in colleges do not have either an M.Phil. or Ph.D. degree.
- There is only one computer for 229 students, on an average, in colleges.

The quality gap presented in Table 9.13 is an eye opener. According to Thorat, there are mainly two reasons for this quality gap: (i) availability and quality of facilities and (ii) quality of faculty. The key factor behind quality gap is the under investment in higher education since the 1980s. Several colleges and institutions have been established as self-financing institutions during the last two decades. No doubt these institutions have created large number of additional seats in various disciplines in higher education. However, majority of these institutions are in short of quality faculty. They are running on 'surrogate' faculty (Chauhan, 2007).

CONCLUSION

Indian higher education system suffers from wide disparities on regional (i.e. inter-state disparity), social (i.e. general, SCs and STs), economic (poor and non-poor) basis. It also suffers from yawning gap in funds, as well as from archaic

TABLE 9.13

Quality Gap in Indian Higher Education System

	Degree of all Universities/ Colleges	*Bench mark (As 'A' Grade Universities/Colleges)*	*Quality gap*
(1)	*(2)*	*(3)*	*(4)*
Universities			
Departments (per university)	29	34	5
Sanctioned faculty (per university)	287	432	145
Filled up faculty position (per university)	220	329	109
Faculty members with Ph.D.	158	432	274
Number of teachers (per Department per university)	8	10	2
Number of books in a library	2,88,913	3,52,886	63,937
Colleges			
Student-teacher ratio	27	20	7
STR (for permanent teachers)	33	30	3
Teachers (per college)	47	3078	31
Permanent teachers (per college)	39	54	15
Ad hoc teachers (per cent)	9	25	16
Books (per college)	11,966	15,215	3249
Journals (per college)	13	22	9
Students (per computer)	229	145	84

Source : "NAAC Report", *Indian Express*, June 9, 2007.

regulatory mechanisms, poor quality, and low efficiency. One of the biggest problems of social equity in India arises from the poor access of higher education to the common man. It is reflected in Gross Enrolment Ratio, which is amongst the lowest in the world. This is perhaps due to the mistaken notion that universal literacy is adequate for the masses and higher education is meant only for the elite. However, a much higher GER of about 40-50 per cent is a need of the hour to make India knowledge society, which is a fundamental requirement of a rapidly growing Indian economy. If this is not done properly on priority basis, the large number of young people entering the working age group will not be able to convert them into human capital. Thus, India will not be able to reap the fruits of the so called 'demographic dividends'.

The Government has a sole responsibility to provide basic education to all its citizens and also make them efficient and skilled workers so that they will contribute to nation-building. Because of rising cost of higher education and increasing needs of it, it appears that public funding is not sufficient to meet the growing demands of higher education in view of the pressure on fiscal deficit. Public-private partnership is the only viable solution in this regard. A tactic shift in the higher education system in India has become extremely urgent. A strong and coherent framework for regulation must replace the current system of multi-regulatory bodies which have created confusion and plethora of constrictive rules.

There is a need for consolidation and upgradation of universities and colleges, keeping in mind the requirements of the industry and other sectors of the economy, competitive practices must be allowed to make the system market-oriented. Non-marketing education streams must be protected. Regulatory framework should ensure that new monopolies and cartelization mechanism are not created. In view of the existing regional-social-economic disparities in the higher education, target-oriented efforts are required for the expansion of higher education institutions in the areas. Higher education should be accessible to the whole of the society. Hence, to make it affordable is a must. Quantitative growth along with high quality of higher education will make the higher growth of the Indian economy more sustainable in the long-run.

References

Agarwal, Pawan (2008) "Towards Excellence: Higher Education in India", Working Paper No. 178, Indian Council for Research in International Economic Relation.

Bhagat, Rashida (2007) "India's Dismal Record on many Front", *The Hindu Business Line*, New Delhi, Dec. 12, p. 8.

———, "Out of School—An Elementary, Unaddressed Problem", *The Hindu Business Line*, New Delhi, June 1.

Bharadwaj, Sanjeev and Dev, Manish (2007) "Commercialisation and Privatisation in Indian Higher Education System in Relation to Quality", in Meenu Agarawal (ed.), *Education in Third World and India*, New Delhi, Kanishka Publishers, pp. 346-55.

Chauhan, Shyam Sunder Singh and Gupta, Sangita (2007) "Access and Equity in Indian Higher Education System: Problems and Prospects", in Meenu Agarawal (ed.), *Education in Third World and India*, New Delhi, Kanishka Publishers, pp. 329-45.

Government of India (2006-07) *Annual Report, 2006-07*, New Delhi, Ministry of Human Resource Development.

———, (2002) *Tenth Five-Year Plan, 2002-07*, Vol. III, New Delhi, Planning Commission.

———, (2008) *Eleventh Five-Year Plan, 2007-12*, Vol. I, New Delhi, Planning Commission.

NAAC (2007) "Assess of the Higher Education", New Delhi, National Assessment and Accreditation Council, UGC, Ministry of HRD.

Pai, T.V. Mohandas (2008) "Key Note Address on Creating India's Tomorrow—The HR Challenge", *The Hindu Business Line*, Cheenai, April 12.

Thorat, Sukhdeo (2006) 'Higher Education in India: Emerging Issues Related to Access, Inclusiveness and Quality", Nehru Memorial Lecture, University of Mumbai, November 24.

Tilak, J.B.G. (2006) "Quota in Higher Education: Must Not in Perpetuity", *The Hindu Business Line*, New Delhi.

10

Equity in Higher Education

SANJUKTA DAS

INTRODUCTION

Since the Presidential address of T. Schultz in the American Economic Association in 1960, education is viewed as an important form of investment. Highly educated people earn more and also are the productive assets. They help to raise GDP of the country and GSDP of the state. Government spends and is expected to spend a significant proportion on education to achieve higher economic growth. But the Government should spend the right amount (and proportion) and on the right category to achieve efficiency, equity and optimality.

The problems of Indian education center on financing, equity in access, excellence and out-turn. As these problems have been confounded by the rapid speed of globalization under which society needs only educated manpower; the deprived in India are now victims of double whammy. Their traditional deprivation keeps them away from education. The demands of a knowledge-driven society under globalization leave them out of the mainstream as social misfits as they lack education (Radhakrishna, 2006). In this regard, some of the important questions are: What is the amount and share of public fund that is invested in higher education? Who gets what types of higher education? Does this present system of education lead to equity or not? This paper makes a modest attempt to deal with some aspects of these questions taking the case of higher education in Orissa.

HIGHER EDUCATION IN THE COUNTRY AND IN THE STATES

India's gross expenditure on education, by the state and Central governments combined together, is nearly Rs. 1 lakh crore or 3.52 per cent of the GDP. The Government of India's spending on education is expected to rise to six per cent of the GDP by 2009-10. Higher education accounted for 15.6 per cent of the total educational spending in 1981-91, which declined to 9.77-10.97 per cent in the Nineties. However, expenditure on higher education as per cent of GDP is rising (from 0.34 in 1981-91 to 0.60 in 2000-01) over the years (Kapur and Mehta, 2004). However, the Government's expenditure on higher education per pupil in real terms is declining during the last two decades even if the total expenditure is rising over time (Tilak, 1997). State governments also spend on education, it being in the concurrent list. Among the states, in 1996-97, Delhi spent 31.12 per cent (highest) of its budget on education while Sikkim spent 5.55 per cent (lowest). Orissa was spending 23.76 per cent of its budget on education. Within the education sector inter-sectoral allocation varies from state to state. Delhi was spending 2.28 per cent on higher education and 6.41 per cent on technical education while the allocation of Andhra Pradesh for the same was 19.84 and 2.87 per cent respectively. Orissa was an average state with allocation of 14.70 and 3.06 per cent for these sectors.

Despite the growth of higher education, the overall share of graduates in the 20-24 age-group population in India is about 8 per cent (2001 Census). It has only about 8 to 9 per cent of its relevant age group enrolled for higher education, as against 50-85 per cent in developed countries. India's gross enrolment ratio (GER) is higher than that of the developing countries average but lower than Asia (11 per cent) and much lower than the OECD countries (Kapur and Mehta, 2004). There is considerable inter-state variation in the level of higher education. According to NSS 2003 data, while the GER in higher education at aggregate level is 13.22 per cent, it is more than national average in states like Nagaland (38.6 per cent), Goa (27.3 per cent), Kerala (24.2 per cent), Manipur (24.7 per cent), Himachal Pradesh (20 per cent) and Jammu & Kashmir, Tamil Nadu and Pondicherry (with 18 per cent). The GER is lower than the national average in states like Tripura (3.2 per cent), Assam (6.6 per cent), Meghalaya (7.2 per cent), Chhattisgarh (7.6 per cent), Orissa (8.2 per cent), Jharkhand (10.3 per cent), West Bengal (9.7 per cent), Bihar (10 per cent), Sikkim (10.8 per cent), and Rajasthan (11 per cent). The enrolment ratio based on eligible student (ERE) is an useful estimate as it indicates the access to education to those who have completed the higher secondary stage. In 2003-04, about 59 per cent of those who completed higher secondary entered the higher education stream. These ratios are higher than the national average by substantial margin in Mizoram (87.1 per cent), Manipur (87.7 per cent), Nagaland (85.6 per cent), Jammu & Kashmir (76.6 per cent) and Kerala (70.6 per cent). By national comparison the ratio is much lower in Tripura (37.8 per cent), Chhattisgarh (49.6 per cent), Orissa (50.2 per cent), and Arunachal Pradesh (53.5 per cent). In rest of the major states the ratio was close to the national average of 59 per cent.

Female graduates constitute a lower percentage of the total compared to male both at the national and in majority of the states. The exceptions are Meghalaya and Tripura where females outnumber males both in number and per cent while in Orissa females lag behind the male. In 2002-03, Orissa had 345,113 students in higher education of which women's share was 35.69 per cent.

About 2/3rd of the students are found in arts and science streams; commerce and management have 20 per cent; the rest belongs to technical degrees (UGC, 2002-03). This implies that higher education is in the state's domain (as general arts, science departments are not privatised). But there is growing privatization of higher education in the country as well as in Orissa. Privatisation is more prominent in technical education like engineering and medical. At the national level, out of the total 198 medical colleges 44 per cent were private and out of 1202 engineering colleges 84.03 per cent were in private sector in 2003. Privatisation is highest in Andhra Pradesh (>90 per cent) and least in Assam (0 per cent). In Orissa, 86.36 per cent of the engineering colleges are private while only three medical colleges are government. Together they constitute 80.85 per cent.

EQUITY IN HIGHER EDUCATION

Equity in education implies equal access to education. Equality of opportunity is a fundamental right ever since the Constitution was adopted and at present we have free and compulsory education bill. Despite all these the access of the poor to education and especially to higher education is very low. If access to quality education is considered, their share falls further. The website of the Foundation for Academic Excellence and Access (http:// www.faeaindia.org) provides that in India there is a chasm between what the education system is expected to achieve and what it is, in fact, accomplishing, and each of its main objectives remains to be accomplished. Though education should be the medium through which equality of opportunity is to be made concrete, yet it remains an endlessly deferred dream for many.

According to the 2001 Census, the overall share of graduates in the 20-24 age-group in India is about 8 per cent. Of the six categories into which the Census 2001 has classified the Indian population, the degree holders in the 20-24 age group account for only 2.3 per cent and 3.6 per cent among the Scheduled Tribes and Scheduled Castes respectively. Among the religious groups it is 4 per cent for the Muslims, 7.4 per cent for the Buddhists, 7.6 per cent among the Sikhs, 9.8 per cent among the Hindus (Hindus excluding the SCs and STs), and 11 per cent among the Christians.

Here under equity, access of the rich and the poor to quality education for general and technical education is analysed. Intentionally we have not attempted the rural-urban and the male-female divide with regard to the access to higher education. The rural-urban analysis is avoided as institutions providing higher education are located mainly in the urban areas and children of the rural areas also come and study here. In GER (HE) this fact will be ignored. It is a fact that females lag behind male in all types of educational access. This is because of the household's differential rates of return from son's and daughter's education (Becker and Tomes, 1976; Rosenzweig and Schultz, 1982; Subramanian, 1995; Rose, 2000). But with increase in household income both son's and daughter's higher education is pursued. Thus, we find difference in the economic condition as the root cause of the differential access. There are significant differences in enrolment rate among the poor and non-poor in the country. According to Thorat (2006), in 1999-2000 the GER in higher education for the poor was 2.4 per cent as against 12.91 per cent for non-poor, the average being 10.10 per cent. The GER for the poor was almost 12 times lower compared to the non-poor. Within the poor, however, the GER was the lowest among the poor belonging to ST and SC category, followed by OBC and others. The GER for poor belonging to ST, SC, OBC and other is 1.55 per cent, 1.89 per cent, 2.30 per cent, and 3.58 respectively.

Now, with industrialisation and the advancement of the economy, privatization and globalization, there is growing private demand for education which is a mixed good. People are revealing their preference for quality education. They are even willing to pay higher amount for private education when they are combined with personal care, invigilation and thus differentiating it from education imparted in the government institutions. But majority of the poor cannot afford for such facilities. Very often they also do not have such information. They enroll their children in the government or private schools of traditional type where facilities are poor in terms of teacher quality, teacher-pupil ratio, teaching equipment etc., where no personal care is taken. This results in the difference in quality of education received by the rich and the poor and the difference in their performance and achievement. The process which starts at the primary school level continues and accentuates at the higher stages resulting in iniquity. Inequality in general and technical education at the tertiary level is discussed in detail in the following sections.

GENERAL EDUCATION

In general education, a number of colleges and universities are imparting teaching at the graduation and the post-graduation level. Quality of teaching of these institutes vary quite a lot, arising from the number of qualified staff, salary of the staff, good library facility, type of management, etc. In a broad way, quality of the institutes of the urban areas can be taken as superior to those of the rural and semi-urban areas. Again within the urban areas, there are hierarchies. Children of the poor households in the rural areas cannot afford for the cost of staying in the hostels and reading in good institutes. They pursue their studies in their local areas.

In these days of liberalisation and globalisation with more emphasis on industrialisation and technological advancement and especially with the growth of information technology (IT), a majority of the meritorious students, especially among the boys, are not showing interest for general education in Orissa. Consequently, only the girls and less meritorious boys and children of poor households are coming for general education. This is because of the declining scope of job opportunities for the students pursuing general education. Again in general education, courses like MBA, MCA, MFC, etc. are able to attract students where the probability of job opportunity is higher compared to others. Universities and colleges are offering these courses under self-financing schemes and are charging high fees. The poor households are not able to go for such huge investments because of low income and low risk bearing capacity even if banks are offering education loans for such courses. Of course, some of the lower-middle class households are investing in such ventures without knowing the real expected average earning, variance and beta. The rich households because of their high income and risk bearing capacity are enrolling their children in these self-financing courses. Students from poor households are either going for general education or they do not enroll in any course. In fact, in many Social Science and Humanity Departments, seats are lying vacant while the gross enrolment ratio in higher education is just 11 per cent in the country and much less in Orissa. Thus, at present there is increasing scope for the rich to have better employment opportunities and very less or no opportunity for the poor.

TECHNICAL EDUCATION

In technical education too, there is marked difference in quality in government and private technical institutions. Excellent institutions in the former category are the IIM and IITs. The KIET and Manipal Institute of Technology belong to the latter category. They are found both inside and outside the state. The reservation system has been introduced for mainstreaming the weaker section in higher education and especially in technical education. But this is applicable for the government or government-aided institutions. Again it is found that the students who benefit from such reservation system mostly come from the creamy layer as it requires at least minimum level of information and performance and spending. All taken together it requires economically good family background. Students of the rich households when do not get a seat in the good technical institutes, manage to get it in private institutes by paying high fees and secure their future. In the job market, certificates from the good institution are valued high. Reputed companies come to these institutes for campus selection. Thus, the same or even higher standard students reading in mediocre category government institutions do not get the chance of such selection. Private companies generally go for campus selection as it is less costly compared to the recruitment through open advertisement. In case of appointment through open advertisement, the chances of getting an appointment for a student of other institutions (other than the above mentioned) cannot be ruled out. Thus, appointment through open advertisement at least provides a scope for job to the poor students. Moreover, the children of the rich households, educated from technical institutes, when do not get appointment in the campus interviews again move to the metros and try there for some time. This requires information as well as huge expenditure since often this waiting time very is long. But, finally they get settled in high paid jobs or high earning self-employments.

Emerging Problems

Increasing industrialization and technical advancement in the Indian economy and the opening up of the world market have increased the employment opportunities of the technically-educated people. This has created a craze among the students to have technical degrees. Realising the good profit prosperity, private sector has come up and has established a number of such private institutions in the country. These private institutions are charging exorbitant amount of fees which the poor households are not in a position to afford and reap the benefits. In Orissa, there are more than 60 engineering colleges. The incentive for technical education has gone so high that a number of coaching institutions with residential facilities have emerged to provide coaching only for the entrance examination of the technical education institutions. Most of the lower and upper middle class and upper class parents of +2 science pass students enroll their children in such coaching institutes for one to two years bearing huge expenses. Moreover, they are often spending a lot in admitting their wards in such technical institution under payment seats (even by incurring loans) with the hope of getting good salaried jobs. The poor households are not able to compete in such race and lag behind.

The present trend of liberalization has not only brought a gloomy future for research in traditional subjects by diverting students to technical and non-traditional types, it has also brought a number of issues which need serious attention. Some of them are discussed here. We have adopted liberalisation, globalisation and privatisation policy to have better resource allocation and to improve efficiency, economic growth and standard of living along with reduction of poverty. Freely competitive economy is considered to be the Pareto optimal as it maximizes consumers' satisfaction, producers' profit and optimizes overall resource allocation. All these are true; but since the factors of production are unequally distributed it may not bring equity. The market economy has the inherent tendency of enlarging inequality as factor rewards are based on marginal productivity which is high when a factor is scarce. Thus, some sort of redistribution function of the Government is required which Musgrave categorises as the 'distribution function' of the Government. But the reality of our so-called liberalised economy is: (1) the existence of asymmetric information, (2) large selling cost in the form of advertising, and (3) overall not the perfect competition as such, rather monopolistic competition or oligopolistic competition. The so-called private technical institutions spend huge amount in advertisement and glamourise their outcome. They provide only partial and lop-sided information instead of giving the right kind of information. For example, when they advertise that there is 100 per cent placement, the duration of the workers in the jobs and the promotion prospect are not informed. In a perfectly competitive market both buyers and sellers are expected to know the quality and price of the product. But here the investing parents know only little and allocate their resources resulting in inefficiency. Competition is expected to reduce the price. But here liberalisation by increasing the freedom and reducing the restrictions allow the private firms to establish such institutions and charge higher fee and reap huge profit. Is it not the duty of the state to compel such institutes to give right, detailed and authentic information to the public? Should the state reduce restrictions and be the silent spectator of such huge investment by the public, finally leading to crash (like stock market crash)?

There is no manpower planning. Technical institutions are set-up or are allowed to set-up without estimating the requirement of technical personnel. With the notion that in the liberalised world market each one can move to anywhere to receive high payment, institutions are set-up and provide education and training to the students by charging exorbitant fees. In the advertisement—'world class teaching, 100 per cent placement, placement in very good establishments of the world, etc.'—are given without giving details. Only a few selective information like the highest pay, appointment in the most lucrative institution, etc. are revealed/glamourised in the advertisements. In the Nineties when the country experienced stock market crash because of financial sector reform, various regulatory and supervisory bodies like SEBI, IRDA, etc. were established and several prudential measures were introduced. However, no such measures have been taken in this regard. Should we wait for the time for a crash to occur? One thing we should not forget that in case of stock market generally the upper middle class and rich people are the investors. Therefore, the investors at least have the capacity to absorb the shock. But here the lower middle class people who are also spending on their children's education may not have such shock absorption capacity.

The same thing is also relevant for the emerging self-financing courses run by the colleges and universities. The sharp increase in the number of courses and the seats therein create skepticism regarding the job opportunities of the students. The possibility of unemployment for some of these students who might have taken loans for paying fees cannot be ruled out. Moreover, the growing unemployment among the general educated youth due to declining employment opportunities in the public sector is expected to increase. These when taken together can constitute a large section of frustrated youth whose entering into various types of crimes cannot be denied off. The increased crime rate, *bandh* rate and terrorist activities are to some extent the manifestation of the Government's institutional failure in providing or creating employment. This trend is expected to increase further. The youth of the lower middle class households who are investing in such type of human capital formation will feel frustrated when they do not get jobs. They are likely to develop suicidal tendency or revolt against the system or join some unethical and illegal activities like computer hacking, internet crime, etc.

CONCLUSION

In this changed scenario, the role of the welfare state needs to be properly identified. While adopting liberalisation, privatization and globalization policies the state should not sit idle following a *laissez-faire* policy. It should undertake its new and larger responsibility in the liberalised era to create the right kind of institutions for the prevention of such things and to provide right information, insurance facility and enforcing various prudential norms for such parties and prevent such high level of inequity in the society. If the state fails to do so, the system will ultimately bring human and material cost. It is, therefore, better not to sit and watch rather to act from the beginning.

References

http://www.ugc.ac.in/more/chairman_nehru_lecture.pdf

Kapu, D. and P.B. Mehta (2004) "Indian Higher Education Reform: From Half-Backed Socialism to Half-Backed Capitalism", CID Working Paper No. 108.

Musgave, R. (1959) *The Theory of Public Finance*, McGraw Hill, Kogakhusa, Tokyo.

Becker, Gary S. and Tomes, Nigel (1976) "Child Endowments and the Quantity and Quality of Children", *Journal of Political Economy*, 84(4): s143-s162.

Subramanian, Shanker (1995) *Gender Discrimination in Intra—Household · Allocation in India* (mimeo), Department of Economics, Cornell University.

Rosenzweig, Mark R. and Schultz, T. Paul (1982) "Market Opportunities, Genetic Endowments, and Intra-family Resource Distribution: Child Survival in Rural India", *The American Economic Review*, 72(4), 803-15.

Tilak, J.B.G. (1997) "The Dilemma of Reforms in Financing Higher Education in India", *Higher Education Policy*, Vol. 10, No. 1.

11

Economics of Higher Education in Orissa

KISHOR C. SAMAL

Physical capital and financial capital are essential inputs but not sufficient condition for increasing national output. The other inputs are human capital, natural capital and social capital. In the present era of liberalisation and globalisation, human capital is considered to be most important input in the development process of a nation. Particularly in case of Orissa where a higher proportion of people live below poverty line, its share in aggregate state domestic products of all major states in the country is gradually declining since 1991. Economic disparity among the states in India is growing in the post-reform era. Prosperous states have prospered further while the poor ones like Orissa became poorer. The state with greater economic strength has gained at the expense of poor states. The lion's share of forthcoming industrial investment proposals is also moving to industrially prosperous states. In spite of the various industrial policies in Orissa since 1980, there is a process of deindustrialization due to closure of big private sector units, loss-making PSUs, sick state sector establishments and vanishing of SSIs since 1990. Agriculture in the state is in shambles, when farmers are compelled to sell their paddy below the minimum price. Therefore, in this scenario, where physical and finance capital are not moving into Orissa since 1991, the importance of human capital in the development process of the state cannot be ignored. Educational attainment is the major factor in accumulation of human capital. No single nation in the world with illiterate and uneducated people is developed and advanced. The percentage of growth rate explained by education varies from 11 per cent in Asia to around 9 per cent in Europe.

EDUCATION EXPENDITURE IN ORISSA

Financing of education by government is the most important instrument for development of education in a poor state like Orissa to expedite the development process. However, after liberalisation and globalisation in Orissa, between 1990-91 and 2000-01, the real increase in public expenditure on education was only 2 per cent, while the nominal increase during the same period was four times. Orissa spends around 5 per cent of SDP (Table 11.1) though the Education Committee (1966) and the Rammoorthy Committee (1991) recommended spending of 6 per cent on education. The share of education in total budget expenditure during the period 1990-91 and 2000-01 is between 16 to 20 per cent. During the same period, the percentage of revenue expenditure on education was found to be around 20 per cent which is lower than that in Bihar and Assam at 28 and 25 per cent respectively. In spite of this, the Government of Orissa has made the strong argument in favour of reduction of revenue expenditure on education in its White Paper. The White Paper suggests capping the expenditure on education. Though the fees of students in primary and upper primary schools are said to be free, irrespective of the financial condition of the students, the development fees at the rate of Rs. 60, Rs. 150 and Rs. 175 are being collected from each student at various stages. In addition to this, there has been increase in

Table 11.1
Budget and Revenue Expenditure on Education in Orissa

Year	*Budget Expenditure*	*Revenue Expenditure*	*% of total budget expenditure*	*% of total revenue expenditure*	*% of SDP*
1990-91	451.03	441.88	16.45	20.17	4.56
1991-92	539.01	535.01	16.38	20.30	4.21
1992-93	616.96	606.31	16.97	19.89	4.49
1993-94	681.44	674.65	16.75	19.39	4.30
1994-95	811.84	799.12	17.41	19.80	4.28
1995-96	928.38	926.33	18.05	19.72	3.99
1996-97	1065.22	1052.80	17.79	20.34	4.80
1997-98	1195.09	1193.01	18.69	21.55	4.36
1998-99	1461.76	1459.22	18.90	21.41	4.96
1999-2000	1913.77	1906.27	20.67	22.54	6.13
2000-01	1735.72	1717.00	17.95	19.44	5.64

Source : Government of Orissa, *Finance Account* (Various years).

examination fees, fees for giving certificate, enrolment fees, etc. These steps adversely affect the poorer section of the students.

A perusal of data on inter-sector allocation within education revealed that the allocation towards elementary education within total educational expenditure moved within a range of 55 to 58 per cent between 1990-91 and 1998-99 (Table 11.2). It reached to the highest level of 65 per cent in 1999-00, and then decreased to 60 per cent in 2000-01. The share of higher education did not vary much and that of secondary education seemed to have suffered severely in terms of relative allocation after 1994-95. The share of higher education and technical education in the total education expenditure declined from 14.39 per cent and 3.87 per cent in 1990-91 to 12.22 per cent and 1.19 per cent in 2000-01 respectively (Table 11.2).

Though elementary education, the priority area under education, received a lion's share of total education expenditure and grew at 6.68 per cent (at 1993-94 price) more than the

TABLE 11.2
Inter-Sectoral Allocation Expenditure on Education in Orissa (per cent share)

Year	*Elementary*	*Secondary*	*Higher/ University*	*Technical*	*Others*
1990-91	54.87	24.86	14.39	3.87	2.01
1991-92	58.08	22.08	15.04	3.15	1.65
1992-93	58.36	22.60	14.10	3.08	1.86
1993-94	57.23	24.70	13.81	2.20	2.06
1994-95	55.37	23.79	15.77	3.09	1.98
1995-96	54.87	24.64	16.57	2.81	1.11
1996-97	54.59	25.49	15.85	2.70	1.37
1997-98	57.15	24.85	14.67	2.21	1.12
1998-99	55.03	28.50	13.55	1.92	1.20
1999-2000	64.96	22.04	10.94	1.01	1.05
2000-01	59.97	25.42	12.22	1.19	1.20

Source : Government of Orissa, *Finance Account* (Various years).

growth rate of education expenditure, yet it remained lower than two-third norm prescribed by the Education Commission (1966) and the Ramoorthy Committee (1991). This implies that intra-sector allocation within education sector favoured secondary level education at the cost of elementary education. The financial constraints in education have its implication on the performance of education sector in the state of Orissa.

STATUS OF EDUCATION IN ORISSA

The progress of education in Orissa during the 1990s is not satisfactory. The number of new schools established during this period is highly unsatisfactory (Table 11.3). The enrolment ratio, drop-out ratio, student-teacher ratio, per student expenditure, etc. are dismal in 2000-01 compared to 1990-91 (Table 11.3).

1. Literacy

Orissa ranks 24th among the 35 states/union territories in

Table 11.3
Basic Features of Education in Orissa

Features	*Unit*	*1991-92 (if otherwise not stated)*	*2000-01 (if otherwise not stated*
Literacy rate	(%) (1991)	49.09 (2001)	63.61
Primary schools	(nos.)	41,204	42,104
Upper Primary (UP) schools	(nos.)	9,818	11,510
Secondary schools	(nos.)	4495	6165
UP schools to primary schools ratio	—	4.2	3.7
Enrolment in primary schools	(lakh)	36.54	47.10
Enrolment in middle schools	(lakh)	10.53	10.35
Enrolment in secondary schools	(lakh)	7.79	10.83
Drop-out ratio in primary schools	(%)	55.1 (1993-94)	41.8
Drop-out ratio in UP schools	(%)	66.2 (1993-94)	57.0
Student-teacher ratio (primary)	—	37	41
Student-teacher ratio (UP)	—	28	27
Student-teacher ratio (secondary)	—	19	21
Per student budget expenditure at current price (elementary)	(Rs.) (1998-99)	531.8	1480.9
Per student budget expenditure at current price (secondary)	(Rs.)	617.3	3182.49

Source : Offices of various Departments of Government of Orissa.

India in terms of literacy rate in 2001. The overall literacy rate in the state increased by about 15 percentage point, from 49.09 per cent in 1991 to 63.61 per cent in 2001, while many other states could increase much faster. Besides average low literacy rate, there exists significant gender and regional disparities in the state; 50.97 per cent for female, 75.95 per cent for male; highest 80.19 per cent in Khurda district, lowest 31.26 per cent in Malkangiri district. Moreover, as per the NFH Survey in

1998-99 only 20.8 per cent adult male population completed primary level education as against 15.8 per cent in case of female.

2. School Facilities

In order to improve the levels of education of population of a society, provisions of adequate and proper educational facilities are very much necessary. As per the national norms, accepted by the state governments, a primary school is required to be improved in all habitants having a minimum population of 300 and within a walking distance of one K.M. The norm is 200 people in case of habitants located in hilly terrain areas and if it is in case of minority population. The Sixth All India Educational Survey mentioned that there were 73,148 habitations in the state of which 60,289 (82.42 per cent) habitations had primary schooling facilities, leaving 12,859 (17.58 per cent) habitants yet to be served by such facilities within one K.M. of walking distance from the home of the child. The number of unserved habitants was highest (1169) in Koraput district and the percentage was highest (35.40 per cent) in Rayagada district. It is to be mentioned that only 58.92 per cent of primary schools had *pucca* buidings. Less than one-third of primary schools in rural areas had drinking water facilities. More than 85 per cent of schools do not have any facilities for toilet.

3. Pushed Out

As per the national norm, there should be an upper primary school for every two primary schools. Accordingly, in Orissa, for a total of 41,125 (36,306 primary schools and 4819 primary sections attached to other categories of schools) institutions catering primary education in 1993, there should have been 20,563 upper primary institutions (with class VI and VII). But there are only 11,022 institutions (10,259 upper primary schools and 763 upper primary sections). This obviously shows that universalisation of elementary education will be a distant dream in Orissa unless another 9541 institutions are established in the state for the children pushed out of the orbit of upper primary education due to lack of institutions. The ratio of number of upper primary schools to number of primary schools has remained stable at 3.7 for the last several years. Likewise 23.67 per cent of habitations and 13.68 per cent of the population were not served by secondary schools within a distance of 5 K.M. by 1993.

4. Enrolment and Drop-out

The number of students in primary education increased by 18 times between 1947-48 and 1999-2000; in middle level education by 33 times and in secondary level by 20 times. There is a decline in the gross enrolment ratio of girls after 1992-93. In 2000-01, the rate of drop-outs at primary level was 42 per cent and at upper primary level 57 per cent. Many students repeat grades in primary schools due to prolonged absence from school and request from parents to continue their children in the same standard.

QUALITY OF EDUCATION

Education is an important strategy of human resource development. The Das Committee Report in Orissa lays special emphasis on elementary education and intends to cover three major aspects: (i) universal access and enrolment, (ii) universal retention of children up to 14 years of age, (iii) substantial improvement in the quality of education to enable all children to achieve effective level of learning.

Performance of the students depends on quality of learning which are associated with various factors such as teacher-student ratio, teacher's education, teacher's experience, teacher's salary, expenditure per student and facilities (quality school building, library, laboratories, etc.) (Hanushek: 1995; King and Orazen: 1999). Other factors are curriculum, instructional methodology, teacher's training programme, text books, writing materials, amount of time devoted to instruction, father's socio-economic level and socio-demographic characteristics of other students.

EQUITY AND GOVERNMENT RESOURCES FOR EDUCATION

In recent times, particularly in the era of liberalisation and globalisation, there is decline in the state resources on the one hand and increase in enrolment of students and more pressing need for improvement in quality of education (Hughes and Kejariwal: 1993). There is more talk to mobilise private resources, because of resource constraints in the states particularly in a poor state like Orissa. The states have taken various steps to move towards privatization. In Orissa, there has been a move to make some government colleges autonomous, revision of grant-in-code for private colleges and schools, and upward revision of fees in colleges particularly in technical colleges.

On the other hand, general state subsidies for various sectors catering to upper income groups account for seven per cent of the gross domestic product, which is twice the total expenditure on health and education. Moreover, the share of expenditure on health and education has been declining too. In market-related reforms in the era of liberalisation and globalisation the government should take responsibility for creating facilities for and improving education.

Literacy and education help to improve the skill of a person. They have a large and significant impact on growth of productivity. Modern technology is easily adopted by the educated. Spread of technology depends on the earning potential and motivation that are linked to the development of formal schooling. Educational attainment and literacy have another important role in the society as they positively affect efficiency in resource allocation, leading to higher income and more equal distribution of such income. Since education has a strong impact on the individual's earnings, the net effect of the expansion of schooling has been a reduction in the dispersion of earnings and hence a more even distribution of income. However, basic and primary education has the highest impact on distribution of income, favourable to equity (Psacharopoulos: 1988). Hence, there is greater need for the expansion of primary and secondary education (Samal: 1997, 1999). If primary and secondary education is provided under market conditions, as argued by the government in this era of liberalisation and globalisation, only those who can afford to pay tuition fees would benefit. Not only there would be underinvestment on human capital from social point of view but income inequality too would continue from one generation to the next since education is itself a determinant of life time income.

Hence, full subsidization of primary and secondary education is justified. The question of government withdrawing from this sector in the name of non-formal education does not arise at all. The government, instead of NGO and private sector, should take the full responsibility of primary and secondary education. Of course, the issue, in the present context of liberalisation, is whether higher education should be subsidized, to what extent and how? In a poor state like Orissa, full subsidization of the cost of primary and secondary education must be assured before thinking of reduction of grants and subsidies to higher education in the name of privatization of source of educational finance. Again, before withdrawing grants and subsidies to higher education, government must stop general state subsidies to other sectors.

The argument advanced in favour of privatization are unacceptable for a poor country like India and more so in a poor state like Orissa. Of course, education is a merit good from which the community benefits to a large extent and, therefore, it is argued that the community should assume the major responsibility of financing higher education. But community involvement in education, as prevalent in USA and other advanced western countries cannot be expected in India and more so in Orissa where about half of the people live below poverty line. Hence, state intervention in education—primary, secondary and higher—is a must in Orissa as well as in India. The relevant issue is the extent of grants and subsidies, and not the complete withdrawal of the state from the responsibility of higher education.

ALTERNATIVE SOURCES OF FINANCE AND EQUITY

If at all, there is genuine financial constraint on the part of the government, there are various other alternatives to recover the cost of higher education, without adversely affecting the equity such as: (i) upward revision of tuition fees along with increase in number of students' scholarship covering fees, mess charge, clothes, text books, etc. and timely payment of the scholarship, (ii) education loan with proper steps for payment of these loans, (iii) graduate tax, (iv) payroll tax, (v) brain drain tax, (vi) education cess, etc. (Albrecht and Ziderman: 1993; Mathew: 1996; Samal: 1982, 1988, 1999; Shatrugna: 1988).

However, all these sources would provide only a small fraction of the total requirement of financing higher education particularly technical education in Orissa as well as in India. Hence, the deficit should be filled by grants and subsidies. While giving grants and subsidies to higher education, various criteria may be taken into consideration. Reduction of subsidies for education could be considered after the withdrawal of all types of general subsidies to different sectors. More grants and subsidies to be given to degree colleges in rural areas and there should be no further opening of government colleges in urban areas for a certain period, particularly in Orissa, where more than 50 government colleges are in urban centres and not a single one in rural areas. Instead of general subsidies to higher education, grants and subsidies should aim at targeting the weaker sections, as the share in public subsidies in education is not progressive (Jimenez: 1986, 1989). Traditional low and uniform price policy for education may be replaced by policies that differentiate prices by types of consumers, such as higher fees for science, medical, engineering and management compared to arts stream.

Literacy and education not only help to improve the skill of a person and thus in growth of productivity but also improve efficiency in resource allocation leading to higher income and more equal distribution of such income. Thus, full subsidization of primary and secondary education and state intervention in higher education is a must in India. The issue is the extent of grants and subsidies and not the complete withdrawal of the state from the responsibility of education. The resource crunch of government for education since 1991 in a poor state like Orissa has adversely affected the poorer sections of the society. This, in consequence, will further aggravate the social inequality as well as income inequality.

PRIVATISATION OF HIGHER EDUCATION: IS IT POSSIBLE WITH ALTERNATIVE SOURCES OF FINANCE?

From ancient time right up to the early stage of capitalist

development, education services were financed by private sources. After the success of the October Revolution in Russia in 1917, the importance of the public sector in providing educational services to the people was realized. Along with structural adjustment programmes and the liberalisation process dictated by IMF/IBRD in the 1980s and the collapse of USSR in the 1990s, there has been much talk about privatisation of education, more particularly of higher education. Privatisation of higher education, in the present day context, refers to increasing privatisation of sources of educational finance.

In India, the public sector bears around 85 per cent of the total expenditure on education (Table 11.4). The expenditure of the education department as a percentage of the total budget expenditure of the Central and state governments is about 10 per cent (Table 11.5). Such expenditure on higher education as a percentage of the total education expenditure declined from 15.25 in 1981-82 to 13.03 in 1991-92 (Table 11.6) and the share of the total expenditure on education has been declining. The states finance more than 90 per cent of public expenditure on education. In Orissa, for example, education expenditure in absolute terms increased from Rs. 79.70 crore in 1991-92 to Rs. 158.80 crore in 1995-96 (Table 11.7). While its support for

TABLE 11.4
Comparative Partnership in Education Expenditure in India

(in per cent)

Sector	*1950-51*	*1980-81*
Government (Centre/state)	57.1	80.0
Local self-government	10.9	5.0
Private	32.0	15.0
Total	100.0	100.0

Source : V.S. Deshpande, "Privatisation of Higher Education: Inevitability, Problems and Remedies", *Journal of Education and Social Change*, Vol. VIII, Nos. 2 and 3, July-Sept. and Oct.-Dec. 1994, pp. 1-11.

education is smaller than that of the states, which cover the bulk of the recurring cost under the non-plan head, the Centre provides substantial funds in the plan outlay.

Table 11.5

Expenditure of Education Department as a Percentage of Total Budget Expenditure of Central and State Governments (Revenue Account)

(Per cent)

Year	*Expenditure of Education Departments only*	*Expenditure of Education Departments together with expenditure of other departments*
1951-52	7.92	7.92
1961-62	11.70	11.70
1971-72	9.38	9.53
1981-82	9.09	10.30
1991-92	11.01	12.58

Source : Government of India, Department of Education, Ministry of Human Resource Development, DPE Studies-2, Budgetary Resources for Education (1951-52 to 1993-94), New Delhi, 1995, p. 7.

In recent times, two conflicting phenomena have been observed, viz. (i) decline of state resources, and (ii) expectation of increase in enrolment (Hughs and Kejariwal, 1993). Because of resource constraints in the states, efforts are being made to mobilise private resources. Thus, there is an increasing reliance on market forces. But reduction in state financial support results in sacrifice of quality, particularly in higher and technical education. Secondly, the state is vulnerable to international donors such as the World Bank, which have begun to dictate the policy of educational finance, as in the case of DPEP in Orissa.

The states have taken various steps to move towards privatisation. In Andhra Pradesh, the privatisation process started in the late 1980s with such steps as the revision of grant-in-aid code for schools and colleges, etc. (Shatrugna, 1986). In Orissa, for example, there has been a move to make some

Table 11.6
Percentage Expenditure of Education Departments of Central and State Governments by Sectors in India

(in per cent)

Year	*Elementary education*	*Secondary education*	*Adult education, Spl. education*	*Technical education*	*Higher education*	*Others*	*Total*
(1)	*(2)*	*(3)*	*(4)*	*(5)*	*(6)*	*(7)*	*(8)*
1951-52	46.11	19.13	5.30	—	11.2	18.24	100
1961-62	39.99	20.80	4.98	—	13.25	20.99	100
1971-72	41.42	29.41	2.03	5.43	12.24	9.47	100
1981-82	43.83	32.33	0.79	4.08	15.25	3.74	100
1991-92	46.30	33.05	1.22	4.32	13.03	2.09	100

Source : Government of India, Department of Education, Ministry of Human Resource Development, DPE Studies-2, Budgetary Resources for Education (1951-52 to 1993-94), New Delhi, 1995, p. 7.

Table 11.7
Plan and Non-plan Expenditure on Education Disaggregated by Level of Education at Current Prices in Orissa

Year	*Elementary*	*Secondary*	*Higher*	*Others*	*Total*
1990-91	244.50	108.11	63.90 (15.02)	8.01	425.52
1991-92	313.00	116.90	79.70 (15.38)	8.60	518.20
1992-93	354.60	137.50	86.00 (14.62)	10.20	588.30
1993-94	408.10	153.50	84.01 (12.79)	11.10	656.71
1994-95 (RE)	486.34	197.22	133.64 (16.17)	9.12	826.32
1995-96 (BE)	533.99	223.89	158.80 (17.14)	9.57	926.25

Note : Figures in brackets show percentage to total education expenditure.

Sources : (i) Government of Orissa, Finance Department, State Budget documents.

(ii) Shakti Padhi, District Primary Education Project (India): State Finance for Education: Orissa, Bhubaneswar, NCDS, 1996.

government colleges autonomous and revise upwards the fees of government engineering colleges, for example.

There are various options for financing higher education (Mathew: 1996), viz., (i) public financing (through budget provision) and public production (for example, government colleges), (ii) public financing and private production (for example, government-aided private colleges), (iii) private financing and private production (for example, self-financing private engineering colleges). Privatisation of higher education, in the present context, means increasing reliance on private sources for educational finance in place of government grants and subsidies.

SUITABLE CRITERIA FOR GRANTS AND SUBSIDIES

While giving grants and subsidies to higher education in a poor country like India the following criteria could be taken into consideration.

1. General Subsidies

Reduction of subsidies for education could be considered only after the withdrawal of all types of general subsidies to different sectors which constitute about 7 per cent of GDP of India and serve the upper segments of the society.

TABLE 11.8
Rate of Return to Education in India

Year	*Primary*	*Social Secondary*	*Higher*	*Primary*	*Private Secondary*	*Higher*
1995	13.14	16.5	10.3	17.3	18.8	16.2
1998	29.3	13.7	10.8	33.4	19.8	13.2

Source : J.B.G. Tilak, *Education for Development in Asia* (New Delhi: Sage, 1994).

2. Rural

More grants and subsidies to degree colleges in rural areas and no further opening of government colleges in urban areas for a certain period, particularly in Orissa, where more than 50 government colleges are in the urban centres alone and not a single one in rural areas.

3. Informal Education and Training

Since employment in the informal sector is far higher than in the formal sector, grants and subsidies for informal education and training (for example, on-the-job training of apprentices) should be taken into account while subsidizing higher education.

4. Targeting

Instead of general subsidies to higher education, grants and subsidies should aim at targeting the economically weaker sections, as the share in public subsidies in education is not progressive, that is, not proportionately higher for students in the lower socio-economic group (Jimenez: 1986).

5. Differential Prices

Traditional low and uniform price policy for education

should be replaced by policies that differentiate prices by types of consumers (Jimenez: 1989), such as higher fees for science, medical, engineering compared to the arts stream.

Literacy and education help to improve the skill of a person. They have a large and significant impact on the growth of productivity. Modern technology is easily adopted by the educated. Spread of technology depends on the earning potential and motivation that are linked to the development of formal schooling. However, the rate of return is highest in primary education, followed by secondary and then university education. In India, the social rate of return is 29.3 per cent in primary education compared to 10.8 per cent in university level education (Table 9.8).

Educational attainment and literacy positively affect efficiency in resource allocation, leading to higher income and more equal distribution of such income. Since education has a strong impact on the individual's earnings, the net effect of the expansion of schooling has been a reduction in the dispersion of earnings and hence a more even distribution of income. However, the equity effect depends on the level of expansion of schooling. Basic and primary education has the highest impact on distribution of income, favourable to equity, while the equity impact of expansion of post-graduation may equally be negative (Psacharopoulos: 1988). Therefore, there is greater need for the expansion of primary and secondary education (Samal: 1997). If primary and secondary education is provided under market conditions, only those who can afford to pay tuition fees would benefit. Not only would there be underinvestment on human capital from the social point of view but income inequalities too would continue from one generation to the next, since education is itself a determinant of life-time income (Psacharopoulos and Woodhall, 1995)

Therefore, state intervention in higher education is a must in India. The relevant issue at present is the extent of grants and subsidies and not the complete withdrawals of the state from the responsibility of higher education by surrendering to the private sector and so-called self-financing colleges working for profit, which would conflict with the welfare as well as the development role of the state.

References

Albrecht, Douglas and Ziderman, Adrian (1993) "Student Loans: An Effective Instrument for Cost Recovery in Higher Education", *The World Bank Research Observer*, Vol. 8, No. 1, Jan., pp. 71-90.

Deshpande, V.S. (1994) "Privatisation of Higher Education: Inevitability, Problems and Remedies", *Journal of Education and Social Change*, Vol. VIII, Nos. 2 and 3, July-Sept. and Oct.-Dec., pp. 1-11.

Elizabeth, King M. and Peter, Orazen F. (1999) "Evaluating Education Reform: Four Cases in Developing Countries", *The World Bank Economic Review*, Vol. 13, No. 3, pp. 409-13.

Government of Orissa. *Finance Account* (Various years).

———, *State Budget documents*, (Various years).

———, *Economic Survey*, (Various years).

Government of India, Department of Education, Ministry of Human Resource Development, (1995), DPE Studies-2, Budgetary Resources for Education (1951-52 to 1993-94), New Delhi.

Hanushek, Eric A. (1995) "Interpreting Recent Research on Schooling in Developing Countries", TWBRO, Vol. 10, No. 2, pp. 227-40.

Hughes, Rees and Kejariwal Shrawan (1993), "Reflection on Trends in the African and Indian Financing of Higher Education", *Journal of Education and Social Change*, Vol. VII, No. 1, April-June, pp. 9-19.

Jimenez, Emmanuel (1986) "The Public Subsidisation of Education and Health in Developing Countries: A Review of Equity and Efficiency", *The World Bank Research Observer*, Vol. 1, No. 1, Jan., pp. 111-29.

———, (1989) "Social Sector Pricing Revisited: A Survey of Some Recents Controversies", in Proceedings of the World Bank Annual Conference of Development Economics, 1989, pp. 109-38.

Mathew, E.T. (1996) "Financing Aspects of Privatization of Higher Education: Issues and Options", *Economic and Political Weekly*, Vol. XXXI, No. 14, April 6, pp. 866-69.

Musgrave, R.A. and Musgrave, P.B. (1989) *Public Finance in Theory and Practice*, Singapore: McGraw Hill.

Padhi, Shakti (1996) *District Primary Project (India): State Finance for Education*, Orissa, NCDS, 1996.

Psacharopoulos, George (1989) "Education and Development: A Review", *The World Bank Research Observer*, Vol. 3, No. 1, Jan., pp. 99-116.

Samal, Kishore (1982) "Brain Drain Tax: Compensating Developing Nations", *The Economic Times*, June 26.

———, (1988) "Case Against Privatisation", *Mainstream*, Vol. XXVI, No. 40, July 6, pp. 25-28.

Samal, Kishore (1997) "Features and Determinants of RNFS in India and Orissa: A Survey", *Journal of Indian School of Political Economy,* Vol. 9, No. 1, January-March, pp. 65-92.

———, (1999) Privatisation of Higher Education: Is it Possible with Alternative Sources of Finance?" *Man and Development*, Vol. 23, pp. 155-62.

Shatrugna, M. (1988) "Privatising Higher Education", *Economic and Political Weekly,* Vol. XXIII, No. 50, Dec. 10, pp. 2624 and 2626.

Tilak, J.B.G. (1994) *Education for Development in Asia,* New Delhi, Sage.

12

WTO and Higher Education : Challenges and Opportunities for India

NIGHAT AHMAD

INTRODUCTION

The WTO which came into existence a decade ago is a landmark in the development of international trade relations across the world. Replacing GATT it promises better integration of world economy, perceived in terms of opening up of economies, liberal movement of not only goods and services but also knowledge. The WTO thus incorporates trade and services which was not covered under GATT.

GENERAL AGREEMENT ON TRADE IN SERVICES (GATS)

The General Agreement on Trade in Services, commonly referred to as GATS provides an internationally accepted legal framework for promotion of liberalization of trade in services. The basic principles of GATS relate to :

- *Most favoured nation treatment*: no discrimination amongst other members of the agreement in terms of treatment accorded to their service suppliers,
- *National treatment*: foreign services and service suppliers to be treated no less favourably than nationals;
- *Progressive liberalization*: the process of liberalization to be increased especially in view of negotiated commitments, and
- *Transparency*: all policies related to barriers to market access and discriminatory restrictions by the members are to be notified.

The service sector has been classified by GATS into twelve categories, which are further sub-divided into 160 sub-groups. Trade in educational services under GATS has been summarized in Table 12.1.

Those services provided exclusively by the public sector of the country concerned do not fall into the ambit of GATS. Educational systems, especially of higher education of all countries including India are not exclusively provided by the public sector; hence fall under the GATS umbrella. However, it is pertinent to mention here that countries have flexibility to decide in which service sector they wish to provide commitment. If such commitment has not been scheduled, there is no obligation on the part of the country to liberalize its concerned services. The Indian government has not made any formal statement on GATS with respect to education services. Hence, it has no multilateral obligation under WTO to open up higher education services to foreign participation. Foreign participation through twinning programmes, franchises and the like that we witness currently in India has been autonomously driven. But in all likelihood in the near future India will come under international pressure to multilaterally bind the liberalization that has been undertaken in the sector of higher education. Whenever the government decides to include higher education in GATS it must utilize whatever the provisions that

TABLE 12.1

Supply of Educational Services under GATS

Mode of Supply	*Explanation*	*Examples of supply*	*Potential market*
(1)	*(2)*	*(3)*	*(4)*
1. Cross-border supply	Refers to provisions of services that cross the border (consumer does not move)	(a) Distance education (b) Virtual educational institutions	A rapidly growing market
		(c) Education software (d) Training through ICT delivery	Has great potential especially through the Internet
2. Consumption abroad	Provision of service involves movement of consumer to the supplier country	Students going abroad to study	A traditional form. Probably the largest share of the global education market
3. Commercial presence	Service provider establishes facilities in another country independently or through domestic institutions (franchises)	(a) Local university or satellite campuses	Has great potential for expansion
		(b) Language training institutions (c) Private training institutions	Becoming increasingly popular
4. Presence of natural persons	Persons traveling to another country to provide the service	Teachers and researchers working in another country	A potentially strong market given the emphasis of mobility of professionals

Source : Adapted from Larsen and Lancrin: International Trade in Educational Services : Good or Bad?

exist in GATS for exemptions and safeguards. The domestic education system in terms of quantity, quality, costs and equity must be taken into account as also the domestic regulatory framework to safeguard the interests both of the students and the economy at large.

INTERNATIONAL TRADE IN HIGHER EDUCATION

Higher education in the contemporary world has acquired the status of a marketable commodity, its quantity and quality and the fee charged being determined by the market forces of demand, supply and profitability. It is no longer acquired for its own sake, nor is the teaching profession a 'noble' profession that it used to be earlier. The concerns are now related to the 'profitability' of a particular course, with an eye on-the-job market. The teaching learning process has become mechanical and pragmatic. The buyer is willing to pay a premium price for admission to prestigious courses that also promise lucrative job opportunities. The entry of the private sector has necessitated marketing of higher education to attract students, making a good bargain in this process. The 'commodification of education' process is complete.

The entry of higher education in the GATS framework has subjected it to international regulations, negotiations and treaties. While in the past also students crossed national boundaries to acquire foreign education, in the present the same has acquired new dimensions. Export of education services has become an important source of earning foreign exchange. The Australian government quite candidly accepts that revenue from education is 'worth as much as wool and more than wheat', thereby highlighting its importance. In USA educational exports were the fifth largest service sector exports in 1998, and were valued at $11.7 billion (NAFSA, 2000) and contributed over AUS$4.2 billion to the Australian economy (IDP, 2002). A British Council study estimates that Britain could earn up to £13 billion by 2020 from export of education. According to the study education has become Britain's important export industry. Other important countries exporting education are New Zealand, Canada and Germany. Table 12.2 presents the leading exporters of tertiary education in the world. These six countries account for almost 70 per cent of total tertiary level educational exports in the world.

TABLE 12.2
Leading Exporters of Tertiary Education in the World

Sl. No.	*Host Country*	*Year*	*Total No. of Students*	*% of total exports*
1.	U.S.A.	1995-96	453,785	29
2.	U.K.	1996-97	198,839	13
3.	Germany	1996-97	165,977	10
4.	France	1995-96	138,191	9
5.	Australia	1997	102,284	6
6.	Canada	1993-94	35,451	2
	Total		1094527	69

Source : Adapted from UNESCO, 1997, 1999.

The most important market for transnational or cross border education is Asia, which accounts for 76 per cent of students in Australia, 64 per cent in USA, and more than one-third in UK and Germany. A study by IDP Education Australia, 'The Global Student Mobility 2025', estimates that at present there are 2 million students who study outside their home country. This is expected to grow more than three times, to 7.2 million in 2025, with Asia dominating total global demand at 70 per cent.

Table 12.3 presents the number of foreign students from the Asia-Pacific region in tertiary institutions in OECD countries and in United States in 2001. The largest source countries are China, Korea, India and Japan. With growing importance of globally mobile labour, business and knowledge, foreign education particularly in the provider nation is considered advantageous. Study abroad also creates migration opportunities, which is an added attraction for many.

Globally mobile capital and information flow from North America and Europe to Asia, while the flow of people is in the reverse direction. Of the foreign students from Asia-Pacific in

TABLE 12.3
Foreign Students in Tertiary Education from Asia-Pacific Region in OECD Countries, 2001 and in United States 2000-01

Country of Origin	*No. of Students in OECD Nations*	*Proportion of all Foreign Students in OECD Nations*	*Students in US degree granting Institutions*
China	124000	8.5	59900
Korea	70523	4.8	45700
India	61179	4.2	54700
Japan	55041	3.8	46500
Malaysia	32709	2.2	8100
Indonesia	26615	1.8	11600
Hong Kong	23261	1.6	7800
Singapore	19514	1.3	—
Thailand	18172	1.2	11200
Pakistan	10478	0.7	—

Source : OECD, 2003a; Skeldon, 2003.

higher education in OECD countries, 44.3 per cent went to United States, 12.5 per cent to Australia and 11.3 per cent to UK. Approximately 71.8 per cent were enrolled in English-speaking systems.

Study abroad has acquired significance of a different nature. Hence, export of education and removing barriers to its trade is being emphasized in GATS. The USA, for instance, has put proposals before Egypt, India, Mexico, Philippines and Thailand at GATS negotiations in January 2004 regarding removal of prohibitions on joint ventures (in higher education) with local partners. A survey by Edu World (2001) on reasons for study abroad of 1000 undergraduate international students in USA, UK and Australia from ten major Asian sources—China, Hong Kong, India, Indonesia, Japan, Malaysia, Singapore, Korea, Chinese Taipei and Thailand—has brought forth the following responses as shown in Table 12.4.

TABLE 12.4
Reasons for Study Abroad

Reasons for studying abroad	*Proportion of Response %**
Foreign education of better quality	28
Desire to broaden experience	26
Desire to live overseas	23
Foreign education more respected	17
Family pressure to study abroad	14
Course not offered/difficult to enter locally	14
Desire to improve English skills	10

**Note* : Some students have given more than one reason; hence total may not add up to 100.

In considering the choice of destination, the key choice factors were country (54 per cent), course (18 per cent), institution (17 per cent), and city (10 per cent). Three-quarters of the students had friends or relatives in the country of study. International study was financed by the family in 82 per cent of cases, followed by student self-financing (8 per cent) and government scholarships (4 per cent).

The emergence of Asian countries as an important market for higher education is highly significant for India whose several institutions enjoy a good reputation overseas. It is, therefore, relevant to examine the current scenario in higher education in India and explore the possibilities for it in the international market.

PRESENT SCENARIO OF HIGHER EDUCATION IN INDIA

An enormous quantitative expansion in higher education has taken place since Independence with respect to number of institutions, teachers and student enrolment. However, only about 11 per cent of the relevant age group is enrolled in higher education compared to other developing countries, e.g. 20.1 per cent in Thailand, 27.4 per cent in Philippines, 14.3 per cent in Mexico and 11.3 per cent in Brazil.

Higher education is looked upon as the only way to ensure vertical mobility of people in the job market and in society as well. Hence, the massification of higher education with respect to its financing the government has gradually taken over the responsibility almost in totality in accordance with its social commitments. However, the economic reforms of 1991 based on a strategy of liberalization, privatization and globalisation altered the scenario on the education front too, especially of higher education. While earlier higher education was heavily subsidized keeping in view its role in national and social development, in the post-reform period the government began to promote the idea that higher education was a 'non-merit good'. The Ministry of Finance in 1997 prepared a paper on 'government subsidies in India' which characterized higher education as a non-merit subsidy, and sought a drastic reduction in state funding of higher education. It was proposed that over a period of five years, subsidy should be brought down from 90 per cent to 25 per cent. This proposal was further upheld by the Ambani Birla Report (2000), which also recommended reduction in subsidies. This change in government policy was the outcome of the World Bank's advice to developing countries which declared higher education to be a 'non-merit good' in its report "Higher Education: Lessons of Experience" (1994). The World Bank, however, was forced to revise its stand and in a later report 'Constructing Knowledge Societies: New Challenges for Tertiary Education" (2002) in which higher education again came to be classified as a public good.

With the adoption of the reform programme the Government of India began to encourage the private sector to enter this field of activity with almost no restriction. There have been occasions when the government has intervened, with respect to admission as well as fee charged by institutions of higher education. Government financing of higher education has reduced, from 28 per cent of educational expenditure in 1990-91 to only 17.7 per cent in 2003-04. The plan outlay on education has fallen drastically from 7 per cent in the First Plan to only 2.9 per cent in the Tenth Plan. Public expenditure on education has never come even close to the 6 per cent GNP recommended by the Kothari Commission and targeted from time to time. Reduced state funding has resulted in privatisation and commercialisation of higher education beyond the reach and aspirations of the average student. At the same time universities were asked to reduce their expenditure and to seek alternative sources of finance. However, all they did was to raise fees and introduce several self-financing courses. There has been over the last decade or so a proliferation of institutions of higher education in the private sector, especially in the disciplines of medicine, engineering, information technology, business management, hospitality management, tourism, biotechnology, etc. Many sub-standard colleges in engineering and management as well as private universities have come into being and had to be closed down for want of necessary infrastructure.

Another notable development in higher education has been the entry of foreign universities/institutions through twinning programmes and franchises with private educational institutions in India. Countries like USA, UK, New Zealand and Australia are keenly wooing the Indian students and making concerted efforts to market their 'educational wares'. However, none of the top ranking foreign universities are operating in India. Many of them do not have a good standing in their own country. They charge higher fees and their programmes too are of dubious quality. Although the Association of Indian Universities has laid down guidelines for twinning arrangements to ensure genuine partnerships and protect the students, these guidelines are often violated. Sometimes the degrees awarded do not enjoy international equivalence.

The scenario of higher education outlined above is rather disconcerting both with respect to access as well as equity considerations. Only a small percentage of students can afford the higher fees of self-financing courses offered by private institutions or those of foreign universities. A highly elitist form of higher education has evolved. With government gradually withdrawing itself from shouldering the responsibility of financing higher education and the increase in fees in most institutions, equity considerations have been placed on the backburner. Government's objective of establishing a socialistic pattern of society seems to be mere rhetoric so far as its Constitutional commitment towards higher education goes.

CHALLENGES AND OPPORTUNITIES FOR INDIA

Globalization of education under GATS has evoked mixed reactions the world over as also in India. On the one hand, foreign education provides students in developing countries access to modern education and training programmes in diverse disciplines which may not be available domestically. However, on the other hand, the system exacerbates disparities in educational attainment between the rich and the poor students. It is basically elitist. These disparities are enhanced in the form of inequalities in earning capabilities. Higher education provided by foreign institutions enables the developed countries to make inroads into the social and cultural fabric of the recipient country. Sometimes institutions providing market specific programmes are not even universities. They are business enterprises not having their own faculty. They hire contractors to produce and deliver specific programmes. It is also feared that academic independence of educational institutions in developing countries would be jeopardized with not much control over the exporting institutions. The curriculum, standards, faculty and requirements will all be determined by the sponsoring institution and may not always serve the needs of the recipient country. Domestic institutions of higher education, except for the few, will get marginalized in the process. These apprehensions are very real for India in which the majority of institutions of higher education suffer from lack of infrastructure and are starved of funds. Only about 11 per cent of the relevant age-group are enrolled for higher education, the rest being out for a variety of reasons, including inadequate facilities and lack of available seats. There has emerged in India a dual pattern of higher educational development, with a few islands of excellence (the IITs, IIMS and some top medical institutions) in a vast ocean of mediocrity. The conditions are ideal for entry of private as well as foreign institutions of higher education. However, liberalization and globalization of education in itself is not the problem. What is relevant is a supportive regulatory framework to ensure that liberalization is beneficial. An effective registration and certification system is essential to ensure that substandard institutions do not enter and the consumer is protected and well informed. Globalization of educational services should also be seen as an opportunity by Indian universities and higher educational institutions to grow and to rise to world standards and establish their bases in other countries.

Strengths of Indian Education

With its second largest higher education system in the world comprising of more than 400 universities and about 20,000 colleges, including institutions of international repute like the IITs, NITs, IIMs, and medical institutes, India is fast emerging as an important destination for higher education. Some perceived advantages that India enjoys are:

- A strong university network having global recognition.
- English as the language of instruction of all the reputed institutions and universities.
- A diverse cultural exposure that has always attracted the western world.
- Moderate fees and low cost of living.
- Welcoming and safe environment and personal approach.
- Proximity to the Asian market predicted to be the biggest market for higher education in the near future.
- Universities and colleges have been permitted by the Government to reserve 15 per cent of their approved intake exclusively for foreign students. Preference is given to PIO and 5 per cent seats are reserved for NRIs.

Regarding cost of study, Indian universities offer high quality tuition that is more affordable than other educational destinations of importance. For example, average cost of science education for some countries is given below in Table 12.5.

INDIAN INITIATIVES IN MARKETING HIGHER EDUCATION ABROAD

India's potential as a global education destination has now come to be realized. A series of initiatives have been taken by

TABLE 12.5
Average Total Costs Per Course (US $) in Science Including Tuition Fees and Living Costs

Country	*Undergraduate*	*Postgraduate*
India	10,860 (3 years)	10,000 (2 years)
Australia	41,890 (3 years)	29,342 (2 years)
UK	66,660 (3 years)	22,220 (1 year)
US Public	80,872 (4 years)	37,915 (2 years)
US Private	102,758 (3 years)	67,574 (2 years)

the government to tap this potential and to attract more and more international students to Indian institutions, both private and public. Educational Consultants India Limited (Ed CIL) has been set-up as a nodal agency under the Ministry of HRD for placement of foreign students in Indian institutions. Some of the services provided by Ed CIL in the placement of international students are:

- Identifying appropriate course/institutions which meets the students' needs.
- Facilitating determination of eligibility for admission.
- Follow-up with the institutes and sending the students' admission offer letters along with the provisional admission letters received from the college.
- Facilitating/obtaining statutory approvals from the concerned ministries.
- Receiving the students in groups of 5 or more on arrival in India.
- Ensuring with the Institutes hostel accommodation.
- Making arrangement for preparatory courses if required.
- Disbursement of institutional and student costs.
- Acting as local guardian.
- Assisting in departure formalities.

The countries which are targeted are Ethiopia, Kenya,

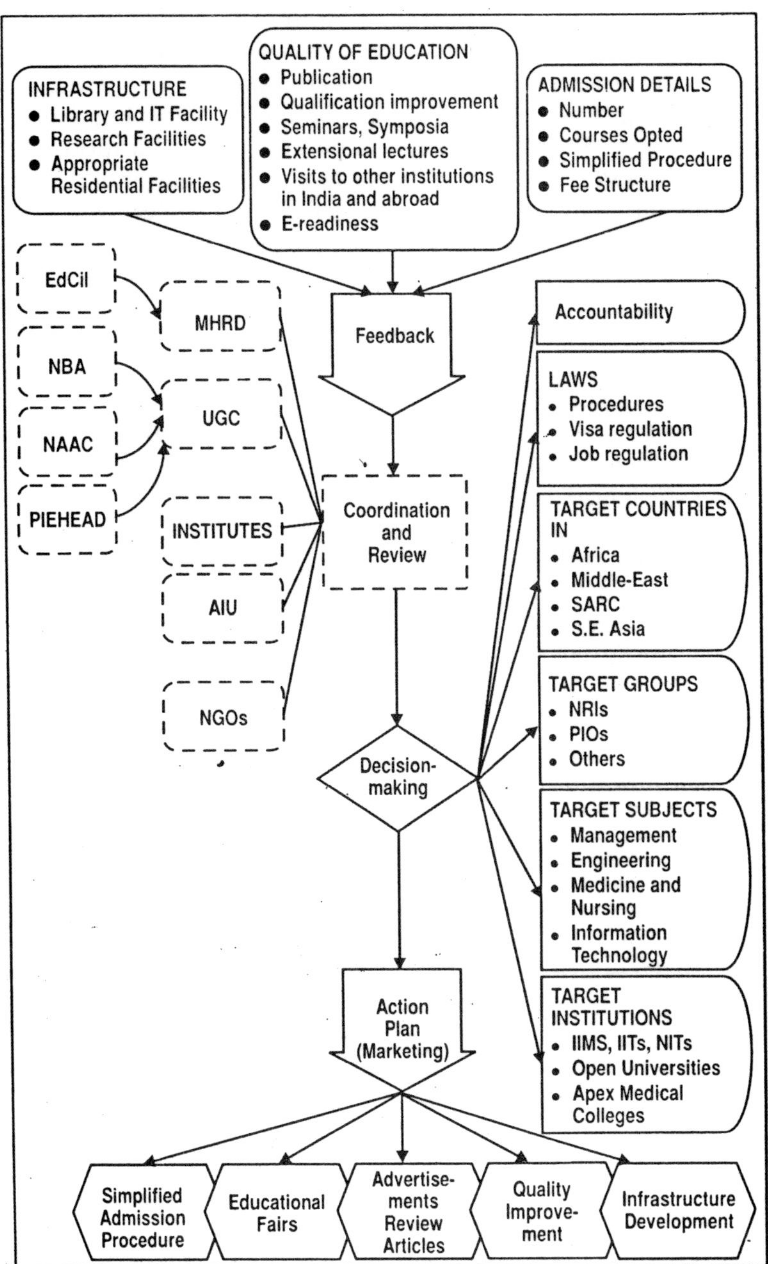

QUALITY OF EDUCATION
• Publication
• Qualification improvement
• Seminars, Symposia
• Extensional lectures
• Visits to other institutions in India and abroad
• E-readiness
INFRASTRUCTURE
• Library and IT Facility
• Research Facilities
• Appropriate Residential Facilities
ADMISSION DETAILS
• Number
• Courses Opted
• Simplified Procedure
• Fee Structure
EdCil
NBA
NAAC
PIEHEAD
MHRD
UGC
INSTITUTES
AIU
NGOs
Feedback
Coordination and Review
Decision-making
Action Plan (Marketing)
Accountability
LAWS
• Procedures
• Visa regulation
• Job regulation
TARGET COUNTRIES IN
• Africa
• Middle-East
• SARC
• S.E. Asia
TARGET GROUPS
• NRIs
• PIOs
• Others
TARGET SUBJECTS
• Management
• Engineering
• Medicine and Nursing
• Information Technology
TARGET INSTITUTIONS
• IIMS, IITs, NITs
• Open Universities
• Apex Medical Colleges
Simplified Admission Procedure
Educational Fairs
Advertisements Review Articles
Quality Improvement
Infrastructure Development

Mauritius, Sudan, Tanzania, Uganda, Bangladesh, Burma, Nepal, Sri Lanka, Thailand, Malaysia, Indonesia, China, Iran, Bahrain, Jordan, Kuwait, Qatar, Saudi Arabia, Syria, UAE and Yemen. As has been mentioned before, in choosing foreign destination students opting for international education have three important considerations—cost, proximity and overlap with their cultural values. In this context India offers a friendly environment, cultural diversity and good value for money to students from SAARC, Middle-East and South-East Asia. It is estimated that India has the potential to afford about 50,000 foreign students in the next couple of years. Presently only about 10,000 are studying in India. The government has launched an exclusive scheme to encourage international students, called District Administration of Students Abroad (DASA) to facilitate entry of foreign students. Further, a Rs. 1500 crore Technical Education Quality Improvement Programme (TEQIP) has been started to upgrade 150 well performing engineering colleges to world class standards. An aggressive marketing and promotional programme has been chalked out by Ed.CIL including advertising, public relations activities as well as recognition of Indian degrees in countries like Malaysia.

The flow chart (on page 177) summarizes the action plan needed for marketing Indian education abroad. It charts out the need for feed-back, the various organizations that are important for coordination and review and the factors important in decision making.

The UGC has initiated a programme for the Promotion of Indian Higher Education Abroad (PIHEAD), for which an expert committee of six members has been appointed to recommend a suitable strategy. Eight disciplines which have a potential for export have been identified, including business management and entrepreneurship, engineering and technology, computer sciences, health sciences, development studies, etc. PIHEAD has planned the following programmes to be taken up in the near future:

- Holding education fairs in selected developing countries with the help of event management companies for marketing of ongoing courses.
- Short-term, non-degree programmes will be designed

and Study in India programmes for marketing in developed countries.

- Designing of promotional materials, such as brochures, multimedia CDs and a dedicated website for PIHEAD.
- Twinning arrangements with foreign universities will be explored.
- Awareness of international education will be raised among all Indian universities and colleges.
- Informal meetings will be held with foreign students in India to gain more input.
- Universities have been approached to submit relevant information to UGC and have been urged to participate in PIHEAD.
- A reputed management consultancy with international exposure will be selected to give a proper direction to marketing higher education abroad.

It is encouraging to know that initiatives have been taken by the government to attract foreign students to India. Considering India's vast potential in this area, a more proactive policy is required. The following measures may be included apart from whatever the government may deem desirable :

- Wide publicity needs to be given to the educational facilities available in India in the reputed institutions of higher education.
- Simplification of admission procedures.
- Clear-cut guidelines related to visa requirements may be provided and the processing of visa applications simplified and expedited.
- Cheap and suitable accommodation should be available for foreign students keeping in view their special needs.
- A special cell may be set-up in universities to deal with the problems of foreign students. It could also be given the responsibility of examining the scope of attracting more foreign students.
- Agreements with foreign countries should be entered

into regarding acceptance of degrees and/certificates awarded by the university.

- A certain percentage of foreign students could be provided with fellowships/scholarships. It is not only through fees that international students provide foreign exchange. Other non-quantifiable benefits arise out of resultant international business connections.

It is essential to have comprehensive data on students' mobility in and out of the country for pursuit of education for any meaningful feedback. The data should include, among others, the number of students, courses sought for, fee structure, curriculum, infrastructure facilities available, teachers' qualification and experience, etc. All major exporters of education meticulously maintain such figures and the details are available on internet for analysis. In contrast, in India there is no single office from where such data could be available. The Government offices which can coordinate for such information could be the UGC, Ministry of Human Resource Development and the Ministry of External Affairs. The data should be regularly exchanged between these offices for appropriate monitoring, evaluation and decision-making. EdCIL can be the central coordinating body for maintaining the statistical data on education.

CONCLUSION

Keeping in view (a) the projected global demand for higher education, with Asia being the biggest market for higher education, (b) the promising returns in terms of foreign exchange, (c) proximity of the Asian market (an important consideration for students), and (d) its own vast infrastructure, India should avail of the advantages and adopt a well planned and well coordinated strategy to promote its educational programmes abroad.

For securing a better interaction with international students, it is important that cultural and social exchanges must accompany academic programmes and should be incorporated in any marketing strategy pursued. Competition will be tough with established exporters of higher education like USA, UK, Australia and Canada. This should not be a deterrent, but a challenge for India to be accepted with a positive attitude. Sincere the efforts will hopefully pay in the long-run. Coordination of different agencies is desirable to make it a success.

References

Ahmad, N. (2005) "Cross Border Marketing of Higher Education", *University News*, Vol. 43, No. 09, February 28 to March 06.

Altbach, P. (2003). "Globalization and the University: Myths and Realities in an Unequal World", *JEPA*, Vol. XVII, No. 2, pp. 227-47.

British Council (2004) "UK to have 30,000 Indian Students in 2020", Rediff.com, April 21.

Gillan, M., Damachis, B. and McGuire, J. (2003) "Australia in India Commodification and Internationalisation of Higher Education", *Economic and Political Weekly*, Vol. XXXVIII, No. 14, April 5-11, pp. 1395-403.

IDP (2002). Education Australia, 2002: Data Base on International Education.

IDP (2002) Education Australia, 2002: The Global Student Mobility 2025.

Larsen, K. and Vincent-Lancrin, S. (2002) "International Trade in Educational Services: Good or Bad?", In *Higher Education and Management Policy*, 14(3), December.

Marginson, S. and Mc Burnie, G. (2003) Cross-Border Post-Secondary Education in the Asia-Pacific Region, Preliminary draft prepared in collaboration with the OECD Secretariat for OECD Report.

NAFSA (2000) Association of International Educators 2000, 'International Education Factsheet". http://www/nafsa.org/advo/facts00.html.

NIPFP (1997) *Government Subsidies in India*, New Delhi, National Institute of Public Finance and Policy, March 1997.

OECD (2003) Cross Border Education: An overview, OECD Report on cross-border post-secondary education, OECD/Norway, November.

Powar, K.B. (2003) "Indian Higher Education in a GATS-Controlled Regime: looking for a pathway in the Haze of Uncertainty", *Higher Education Policy and Practices*, Vol. 1, Nos. 1 and 2, July-September, pp. 1-9.

Prayatna.typepad.com (2004) Exporting education from India: prayatna.typepad.com/education/2004/04/promoting_india.html.

Sahni, R. and Kale, S. (2004) "GATS and Higher Education: Some Reflections", *Economic and Political Weekly*, Vol. XXXIX, No. 2, May 22-28, 2004, pp. 2174-80.

Sify.com: India becomes a global education hub: Sify.com/finance/fullstory.php?id =13456895.

The Hindu (2003), Interview with Australian Minister for Education, Science and Training, May 09, 2003.

UGC-PIHEAD (2004) http://www.ugc.ac.in/new_initiatives/promothe.html.

13

The Implications of GATS Trade in Higher Education Services : The Indian Perspective of Private Participation

D.G. MANNIVANNAN

In 2000, the United States representative to the World Trade Organisation (WTO) proposed the addition of higher education services to the General Agreement on Trade in Services (GATS). Education accounts for $ 2 trillion of the world's economy each year. The higher education services market was estimated in 2002 at approximately $ 30 billion, with the United States holding the largest market share including recruitment of international students, establishment of university campuses abroad, franchised provision and online learning. Higher education was the fifth largest service exported by the US. The General Agreement on Trade in Services (GATS) is currently being negotiated under the auspices of the World Trade

Organisation (WTO). GATS is designed to increase trade liberalisation internationally, and includes education as a service sector. Examples of perceived barriers in the trade in higher education services might include visa restrictions, taxation that disadvantages foreign institutions and accreditation arrangements that privilege domestic institutions and qualifications. Some view GATS as a positive force, accelerating the influx of private and foreign providers of higher education into countries where domestic capacity is inadequate. Others take a more negative view, concerned that liberalisation may compromise important elements of quality assurance and permit private and foreign providers to monopolise the best students and most lucrative programmes.

WHAT IS GATS

The General Agreement on Trade in Services (GATS) covered in the WTO, also a product of the Uruguay Round, is a legally enforceable agreement aimed at deregulating international markets in services, including education. Before this agreement, trade agreements used to be in relation to eliminating tariffs and other barriers for the goods produced in one country and sold in other countries. Some services used to be exchanged but there was no mechanism for trade in services, because they were considered to be place specific and thus non-tradable. The objective of GATS is to liberalise trade in services as quickly as possible. It is clear from the preamble of GATS that it is a multilateral framework of principles and rules for trade in services with a view to the expansion of such trade conditions of transparency and progressive liberalisation and with a desire for the early achievement of progressively higher levels of liberalisation of trade in services through successive rounds of multilateral negotiations. According to the European Commission, the GATS has two components: (1) The framework agreement containing 29 articles, and (2) A number of Annexes, Ministerial decisions, etc., as well as the schedules of commitments by each member government, which bind them to allow market access, and/or remove existing restrictions to market access. This agreement covers all services including education.

WHY EDUCATION IS UNDER GATS UMBRELLA

When the services are entirely provided by the government, they do not fall within the GATS rule. For a service to be out of the purview of the GATS rule it has to be entirely free. However, when the services have been provided either by the government partially or some prices are charged (as happens in education where some fee is charged), or provided by the private providers, they shall fall under the GATS rule. The idea behind this is the creation of an open, global market place where services, like education, can be trades to the highest bidder. GATS cover the educational services of all countries whose educational systems are not exclusively provided by the public sector, or those educational systems that have commercial purposes. Since total public monopolies in education are extremely rare, almost all of the world's educational systems fall under the GATS umbrella. In India, we can get exemption in education from the application of GATS because education at all levels, particularly at higher education level, is not entirely free.

HOW DOES GATS WORK

The 144 participants agree to abide by the basic general obligation of GATS members (e.g., most favoured nation treatment, noted above) and make commitments for specific sectors to eliminate or reduce tariffs and other impediments to trade in services. There is a hierarchy of obligations with general obligations applying to all members, followed by specific commitments specified by each member. National commitments serve as the basis for negotiations between member-countries that are signatories to GATS. The two levels of commitment are:

General Obligation: (e.g., most favoured nation's treatment and transparency). These obligations apply to all services. For example, most favoured nations treatment requires that members extend equal treatment to each other's service suppliers. As GATS members extend equal treatment to each other's service suppliers, the members are entitled to conditions of access equal to the most favourable given to any other nation.

Specific Commitments: These refer to member-country commitments to market access and national treatment for specific castors (such as education). Each government identifies these in its Schedule of Specific Commitments. Government member may make additional commitments to provide access beyond the listed commitments to date have ranged from a few to 120 of the approximately 160 service sectors (including sub-sectors).

NATIONAL TREATMENT : TREATMENT OF GATS PARTNERS IN THE SAME WAY A NATION'S OWN CITIZENS ARE TREATED

Market Access

A negotiated market commitment in specific service sectors. It may subject to various limitations such as number of service suppliers, values of transactions, total number of service operations, total number of people that may be employed in a particular service sector, and limits on participation of foreign capital. Members are free to tailor sector commitments as they wish, as long as the limits are stated at the outset. They may encounter pressure from other members regarding such limitations. Each member may make additional commitments to provide access beyond the listed measures.

Forces Shaping Trade in Education

Education Services Covered by GATS

There are five education services:

- Primary education;
- Secondary education;
- Higher education (including post-secondary technical and vocational education services);
- Adult education (education for adults outside the regular education system); and
- Other education (i.e. testing and certification).

GATS also applies to several ways (modes) of supplying education services:

- Cross-border supply (i.e. distance education);
- Consumption abroad of services by consumer traveling to supplier's country (i.e. students studying abroad); and
- Presence of natural persons from supplying country in consuming country (i.e. faculty teaching abroad).

Governments can make commitments for one area, several, all sectors, or none of them.

Major changes in conditions affecting the context of higher education give GATS a potentially critical role in higher education around the world. These are: (i) globalisation, (ii) improvements in information and communication technology, and (iii) increased competition in higher education.

Globalisation

In today's world, globalisation is rapidly increasing, bringing with it expanded personal mobility; access to knowledge across borders; increased demand for higher education (including e-learning), especially in developing countries, growing worldwide investment; and increased needs for adult and continuing education. As a result the opportunities and capacities to expand the market for higher education have also increased tremendously. The growth will continue even more rapidly over the next few years. With it come both opportunities and potential threats for Indian higher education. Though the impact in the short-run may be limited, the potential long-term consequences are significant.

Information and Communication Technology: The rapid expansion of information and communication technology and the reduced cost of much of this technology have spawned a major expansion in its application to education. In many parts of the world, information technology holds promise for reaching populations that could not be served traditional education institutions.

Increasing Competition: Competition in higher education has increased markedly in recent years in India as policy-makers turn to market forces to reform higher education and reduce costs. Competition from foreign institutions is of special concern to developing nations like ours. We fear that competition from providers in rich nations will disadvantage our higher education system which is under the process of development. If outside providers succeed in recruiting the better prepared and more affluent tuition paying students away from public institutions, they will deprive government-supported higher education of the revenue needed to support public education for poor and less-prepared students. Developing nations like us should be concerned that GATS demands for unrestricted access in the higher education sector will open the door to foreign diploma mills and providers of questionable quality. We have to develop a sophisticated monetary system which will have the capacity to monitor or police these providers. Thus, GATS is seen as hindering their commitments to the public good. The development of a national higher education system essential to national development, efforts to foster national cultural values, promote democracy, and provide educational opportunities for all citizens—not just those who can pay for them.

The education sector is one of the least committed sectors. The reason is not clear, but perhaps it can be attributed to the need for countries to strike a balance between pursuing domestic education priorities and exploring ways in which trade in education services can be further liberalised. Or it could be linked to the fact that to date, education, in general, has taken a very low priority in the major bilateral agreements and rightly or wrongly, the same may be true for the GATS.

Only 44 of the 144 WTO members have made commitments to education, and only 21 of these have included commitments to higher education. It is pertinent to note that Congo, Lesotho, Jamaica and Sierra Leone have made full unconditional commitments in higher education, perhaps with the intent of encouraging foreign providers to help develop their educational systems. Australia's commitment for higher education covers provision of private tertiary education services, including university level. The European Union has included higher education in their schedule with clear limitations on all modes of trade except consumption abroad, which generally means foreign tuition paying students. Only three (USA, New Zealand, and Australia) of the 21 countries with higher education commitments have submitted a negotiating proposal outlining their interests and issues.

THE INDIAN CONTEXT

In fact, universities (*Viswa Vidyalayas*), by definition, have to be international in character. Precedence for trade in the Golden Age of India, Universities at Nalanda, Vikramshila and Takshashila were famous the world over, attracting students from foreign lands. It had at one time about ten thousand resident students and teachers on its roll, which included Chinese, Sri Lankan, Korean and other international scholars. Prior to Independence, affluent students and those who earned a fellowship did go to the United Kingdom (UK) for higher education and returned with a wider world view of things. After independence, students went abroad on Commonwealth and Fulbright scholarships and returned home to transplant their training and experience to the domestic conditions. The latest phase began when (post) graduate students started going to the United States (US) for higher studies with dollar assistantship in their pocket, never to return as if they had entered *Alibaba's* Cave! Of late, there are many Indian students going abroad for undergraduate education as well.

As per Article 1.3 of GATS, government services remain outside the purview of GATS, provided they are not meant for commercial purpose and do not have any competition from private service suppliers. Hence, as per this Article, education does come under the purview of GATS trade liberalisation, since there are already many institutes, colleges, high schools and coaching classes operating in private sector in India. These private service providers are in direct competition with the government-run institutions. Moreover, one should not forget that the leading public educational institutions like the IITs, IIMs and agricultural universities were funded primarily by foreign funds. The shrinking budgetary resources for education are in no way helping the cause of promoting knowledge in India. The per capita total government expenditure on education for 1995 was less than $ 10 per year in India as against $ 1400 in the United States (UNESCO, 1998). The 1990s saw a major turn in the history of contemporary higher education in India. The decade was one of turmoil with an important development being the sustained efforts towards privatization of higher education in India. The financial privatization of higher education, through reduction in public expenditures and the introduction of cost-recovery measures were accompanied by policy measures toward the direct privatization of higher education. A private universities bill was introduced in the Upper House of the Parliament in August 1995, with a view to providing for the establishment of self-financing universities. Mukesh Ambani and Kumaramangalam Birla Committee (2002) strongly suggested that the Government should leave higher education altogether to the private sector and confine itself to elementary and secondary education. But the Committee did not spell out any valid reason. Further, the report urged passage of the private university bill.

Moreover, share of higher education in total planned resources has decreased continuously from 1.24 per cent in the Fourth Five-Year Plan to 0.35 per cent in the Eighth Five-Year Plan (Joshi, 1998). As a result, the state of affairs in the government educational institutions is in dismal condition. Even if the government substantially increases its educational spending via deficit financing, it amounts to an inflation tax. The paucity of funds points out the fact that capital is a scarce factor and human resource an abundant factor in India. Those who go abroad to provide educational services on contractual basis contribute to India's Gross National Product. Similarly, foreign educational institutions operating in India will contribute significantly to India's Gross Domestic Product, and, even more so if the Indian Government stipulates a minimum requirement on hiring of Indian faculty and staff. Hence, private sector participation and trade in educational services seems imperative.

The second classification is based on the nature of trade in (educational) services. Article 1.2 of GATS classifies trade into the following four modes:

(1) Cross Border Supply

It includes courses through distance education, online courses through Internet, educational testing services, and educational materials that are provided overseas. It will also include sale of paperback editions of books and sale of educational CDs.

(2) Consumption Abroad

This refers to import of educational services through movement of the consumers/students to other country for pursuing education. A clear example is that of Indian students studying abroad and spending on educational fees and all related expenses of their stay.

(3) Commercial Presence

It means actual presence of an educational service provider of a country. For example, a foreign university may start a school of journalism in India, giving a foreign degree to the students.

(4) Movement of Natural Persons

As the title suggests, it involves people moving between countries to provide educational services. An Indian teacher going abroad to teach in high schools in US is one such example.

India will have to make, in its communication, specific requests to other countries, propose changes, and indicate its readiness to commit in select types of trade. And, while doing this, India must ensure that the safeguard instruments available in the GATS document are credible and enforceable.

COMPETITIVENESS OF INDIAN EDUCATIONAL SERVICES

For the ensuing negotiations on trade in services, Indian authorities not only need to respond to the proposals and commitments made by others, but put forward India's own proposal and select commitments that are in the best interest of our country. A pre-requisite for that is to generate adequate data on the status of educational service providers and users and its aspects related to trade. Based on that, authorities will be fully able to comprehend India's competitiveness in various sub-sectors of educational services. However, based on the information available at this time, critical observations on India's competitiveness can certainly be made.

Educational Testing Services

The US hopes educational testing services (and training) to

be included in the country commitments. This is not surprising as US already has well established educational testing service providers and they would like to utilise the potential outside the country. India too has a long experience of providing educational testing services. Quality of testing services is well demonstrated by all India qualifying tests such as the CAT (Common Admission Test) of the IIMs, JEE (Joint Entrance Examination) of IITs, NET examination of CSIR-UGC, and GATE (Graduate Aptitude Test in Engineering). If the experience of these services is adapted for various fields, and, if such services can be offered on a year round basis with sufficient computerization and use of Internet facilities, India stands to gain from liberalisation of such services. However, markets for such services will have to be actively sought. Hence, India may commit to liberalise these services, but an adjustment period of at least 6 years is necessary for upgradation and marketing of these services to potential clients. Moreover, willingness of stakeholders to conduct this activity in the private sector needs to be assessed. Only then India can become competitive both in foreign and domestic markets.

Students on Foreign Campuses

In the year 2001-02, 66,000 Indian students had enrolled in different courses in the United States. Currently, however, the number must have gone up. Moreover, there are many more thousand Indian students studying in Europe. A significant proportion of these students would be (post)graduate students on teaching/research assistantships and fee waivers (see Teachers and Researchers Working Abroad below). Moreover, value must be attached to foreign educational experience which certainly widens the horizons of young minds. As far as export of such service by India are concerned, i.e. foreign students coming to India for study, the current prospects are not too bright. However, getting students from developed countries, even from East European countries, would be very difficult as our standards of campus facilities are very poor in general. However, there is a scope for developing high value niche market for some of the programmes that India may offer. Marketing of programmes on education in arts and culture, sanskrit and other languages and literature, and traditional medicinal sciences like Ayurveda could be effectively done by upgrading the campus facilities for some of the specialized institutions in India. A glaring example of this is the programme offered Ayurveda by the Department of Ayurveda at University of Pune. It has twinning agreements with Universities in Italy, Germany and many other countries to send their students here for part of the study. Moreover, there may be niche market for management education as well. India has one of the best management schools in the Asia-pacific region. Indian Institute of Management, Ahmedabad, although does not have any foreign students enrolled in its two-year programme, it has a successful exchange programme for students. More than 45 students go abroad for a term for which they do not have to pay fees. One must also remember that fees in western countries are much expensive than those in India. Promoting such exchange programmes on reciprocal fee-waiver basis will certainly be useful to India both in terms of not losing foreign exchange, and, providing Indian students an opportunity to broaden their worldview. In doing so, Indian institutes will move towards up-gradation of their facilities and infrastructure in the near future. And, with that, the institutes can also attract foreign students for their regular post-graduate programmes in the long-run.

Establishing Schools Abroad

At present, many countries including US are only looking inwards as far as secondary education is concerned. However, Indian proposal should include scope of commercial presence of institutions in the secondary education. India's CBSE system of secondary education is quite robust as compared to the state-board systems. In fact, there are more than 100 (Indian) CBSE schools abroad. With ever increasing Indian diaspora spreading rapidly all over the world, there would be a great demand for CBSE-like schools in UK, USA, Fiji and many other parts of the world. Of course, some initial groundwork will have to be made by identifying and bringing together private providers and the prominent figures from the non-resident Indian community. In the long-run, the school system could be expanded away from the ethnic Indian focus that will be required in the short-run. On the import side, India need not worry much as our system of secondary education is both cost and quality competitive. As far as establishing institutions of higher education abroad is concerned, India's competitiveness is very much in doubt as she needs to address the core issues of capital expenditure requirements. In fact, instead domestic higher education problems should be addressed first to stay import-competitive.

However, one exception must be brought to our notice. The Central Institute of English and Foreign Language (CIEFL), Hyderabad, has successfully launched English Language Teaching (ELT) programme in Kyrgyzstan. The institute won the contract in succession although there was strong competition from other countries (Kolhatkar, 1999). India must capitalize on such experiences and duplicate the efforts elsewhere. As far as presence of foreign higher-education institutions in India is concerned, India should allow it, however, the process of liberalisation must be gradual so that our domestic educational institutions are capable of effectively competing with the foreign institutions. India will need a transition period of at least 6 years to upgrade our campus facilities. Upgrading facilities in all institutions will be difficult. However, selected import-competing institutions must be able to upgrade their facilities. Among other things, these facilities will include availability of course schedules on Internet, telephone registration system for various courses, option for payment of fee through credit cards, well equipped dormitories, classrooms, libraries and sports facilities of international standards, and facilitating growth of off-campus housing infrastructure in the private sector for faculty, staff, and students. Moreover, accreditation system for foreign educational institutions will have to be developed. Indian authorities may need to study how foreign, developed countries governments manage the accreditation system in their own countries.

Teachers and Researchers Working Abroad

Although the annex to GATS mentions that movement of natural persons is excluded from GATS, it clearly provides scope for negotiating commitments on movement of persons in specific services. India must put in its proposal to include commitments on movement of teachers and researchers both at the secondary and higher education level. Already, about 10,000 secondary school teachers are working outside the country for some time. The trend will continue given the scarcity of teachers in developing world and the abundant supply of qualified teachers in India. Nevertheless, there is a need for making projections of export of this educational service. The export of teachers need not be construed to imagine that Indian schools will be deprived of their valuable asset. In fact, a healthy market for teachers will encourage many more to join the profession domestically as well.

Moreover, it must be remembered that many of the Indian (post) graduate students who go abroad for higher studies receive teaching and/or research assistantships and tuition waivers. This is a form of export of educational service in the form of movement of natural persons. The fact that western countries need foreign (post) graduate students to teach independent courses in their universities shows the need for qualified university level teachers abroad.

INDIAN PROPOSALS AND COMMITMENTS

In the light of the above discussion, India must act in self-interest. She must manage to send a proposal and commit to areas where there are strategic opportunities to be exploited through trade. It also entails radical reforms in the domestic educational infrastructure. In this context the following strategies are suggested for India's proposal:

(i) India should endorse the US view of including educational testing services to be included in the country commitments. However, India should ask for phased liberalisation. A lead-time of at least 6 years is necessary to upgrade our reputed testing services to compete effectively with foreign suppliers in the domestic market, and gather market intelligence to focus on adaptation of our services for the export market.

(ii) India may commit to all modes of trade in higher education as well. However, it must be borne in mind that India will have to actively seek niche markets for India-specific knowledge programmes. Moreover, infrastructure upgradation of our premier and import competing institutions must be done on a priority basis so that they can effectively compete with foreign institutions based in India. Again, for this purpose, India must propose for gradual liberalisation. A transition period of at least 6 years is needed to bring our priority institutions on par with the foreign ones in terms of infrastructure and facilities.

(iii) India may make a specific proposal to other countries to commit them for commercial presence in secondary education. This is in view of the proposal that accredited private high schools of CBSE standard stand a good chance to be exported the world over. More than 100 already exist in other countries. Similar US schools exist in India and elsewhere those are primarily meant for non-resident US citizens.

(iv) India may propose for a specific commitment on inclusion of teacher and researcher both at the secondary and higher education level under the trade mode—movement of natural persons. With increasing demand for teachers in the developed countries India may want to ensure opportunities for our human capital. In this context, we have the potential to replicate the experience of CIEFL, Hyderabad, in other educational fields. The commitments will also apply to (post) graduate students who go abroad and earn teaching/research assistantships and tuition waivers. In this respect, India may seek equal pay for these persons, no deduction of social security tax, and no mandatory deduction for teachers/individual retirement accounts. Even if social security tax is deducted, it should be recoverable when a person returns to the home country. Moreover, there need not be penalty for withdrawing money from the teachers' retirement account when one returns to the home country.

(v) Australia, in its communication, has expressed her desire to screen people desiring temporary immigration to Australia. However, she considers restrictions by other countries on foreign equity participation in educational institutions as a deterrent.

These expressions are quite asymmetric in nature. If countries wish to have unhindered entry of their capital in other countries, they must also allow legitimate entry of human capital in their own country. Screening of Indian educationists desiring to temporarily immigrate to countries such as Australia is indicative of protectionist trade policy. Such propositions must be opposed during the negotiations.

(vi) Indian authorities must request for assistance from UNESCO and/or other world bodies for improving educational infrastructure in the country. This has been done in other WTO agreements such as Agreement on Sanitary and Phytosanitary measures (SPS) and Agreement on Technical Barriers to trade (TBT). Moreover, such assistance must be provided in a structured, time-bound fashion. The motivation for such request is that developing countries such as India will find it extremely difficult to cope up with abrupt issues that will arise if commitments were to be adhered to immediately after an agreement is reached. To compete effectively with the developed nations, to upgrade our facilities and infrastructural needs, developing countries must have a transition period of at least six years, after which complete implementation of the agreement can be undertaken.

(vii) For a smooth transition to the new liberalised environment, encourage WTO member-countries to have more student-exchange programmes so that exchange students could become the young ambassadors, messengers and promoters of our educational services in their respective countries.

STRATEGIES FOR DOMESTIC REFORM

(i) Authorities must develop a database on information on all categories of education regarding number of educational institutions, their enrolments (domestic and foreign), faculty strength, financial sources, and quality and accreditations. Further, market intelligence regarding situation in other countries be sought through our diploma attach in the Indian embassies abroad.

(ii) Existing reputed educational testing services will have to be modernized. To compete with testing service such as CAT, GATE, JEE, NET and others must be upgraded and modernized. There is a need to constitute a committee to suggest measures to upgrade these services and to monitor the implementation of the suggested measures. The upgradation will be in terms of year-round availability of the testing service, computer-aided and internet-based testing, and universal acceptability of the tests by various academic institutions including foreign institutions. Moreover, assessment will have to be done whether or not private providers can take on the mantle of running such services for its efficient functioning. Though we are boasting that India is a superpower in IT, in the subject of modernizing our national competitive examinations we have to regret that nothing has been done to make global presence.

(iii) Improvement in the educational infrastructure must take priority. The following items need to be addressed if the infrastructure of import-competing institutions has to be of international standard:

  (a) University course schedules must be available through Internet.
  (b) Automated telephone course registration for every term must be available to students.
  (c) Payment of fees by credit-card should become a standard option.
  (d) Classrooms, libraries, dormitories, sports facilities should be of international standards.
  (e) Off-campus housing arrangements must be facilitated through private sector for faculty, staff, and students.

(iv) Authorities must study the system of regulation and accreditation of educational institutions in foreign countries. Our own accreditation system and laws for foreign institutions must be developed taking into account the treatment given to them in their respective countries. Some of the issues in this connection are discussed here.

REGULATIONS FOR FOREIGN PROVIDERS

As already been stated, a regulatory framework is needed to deal with the diversity of providers and new cross-border delivery modes, and becomes more urgent as international trade increases. In some countries, this may mean a broader approach to policy which involves licensing, regulating and monitoring both private and foreign providers to ensure that national policy objectives are met and public interests protected. It may also involve a shift in government and public thinking while higher education remains a public good, both public and private providers can fulfil this public function. This in turn may introduce greater competition among providers and general confusion for the consumer. Hence, a coherent and comprehensive regulatory framework is called for to serve national interests and protect the interests of different stakeholders, especially students. More work is necessary to determine how national regulatory frameworks are compatible with, or part of, a larger international framework. Increased connectivity and interdependence among nations, as well as liberalised trade, will mean urging greater coherence between national frameworks. How can coherence between a national framework and an international framework actually strengthen national regulatory and policy functions, not weaken them? Clearly there are risks and opportunities associated with this issue but doing nothing is a risk in itself. In April 2003, the All India Council of Technical Education (AICTE), the apex body that oversees the development of technical education in the country, ruled that all foreign educational institutions offering technical education in India will have to register and follow regulations. The AICTE order *inter alia* provides that the foreign university/institution shall be bound by the advice of AICTE with regard to admissions, entry qualification and the conduct of courses/programmes in technical education, as may be communicated to them from time to time.

The well-entrenched and largely self-serving higher education bureaucracy can be expected to come up with more such control measures to check the growth of foreign educational service providers in the country. But given current trends in privatization and liberalisation of the Indian economy, they are unlikely to succeed.

Although India has not made any commitment under the GATS agreement, it negotiated in 1994 to allow foreign colleges. The GATS re-negotiations which were to be concluded by 2005 made this a possibility. Moreover, foreign colleges could come in registered as companies, as in the case of the UK-based Wigan & Leigh—which has established campuses in a number of Indian cities, or, the University of Illinois-linked Quantum Institute in New Delhi.

CREDIT TRANSFER

New types of education providers, new delivery modes, new cross-border education initiatives, new levels of student mobility, and new opportunities for trade in higher education—all this can spell further confusion for the recognition of qualifications and transfer of academic credits. This is not a new issue.

Trade agreements are not responsible for increased confusion, but they add to the complexity and also make resolution more urgent. National and international recognition of qualifications and the transfer of credits has already been the subject of a substantial amount of work. The Lisbon Convention on the Recognition of Qualifications of Higher Education in the Europe Region, the European Credit Transfer System, and University Mobility in Asia Pacific are good examples of regional initiatives that could lead to a more international approach. Association of Indian Universities (AIU) has been accepted as an accredited agency at the national level for undertaking the assessment of foreign academic credentials in India. AIU system must be made more robust and comprehensive and more dynamic in nature to cope up with the increasing demand.

QUALITY ASSURANCE AND ACCREDITATION

Increased cross-border education delivery and a set of legal rules and regulations in trade agreements require that urgent attention be given to the question of quality assurance and accreditation of education providers. Not only is it important to have national mechanisms which have the capacity to address accreditation and quality assessment procedures for the academic programmes of new private and foreign providers, it is equally important that attention be given to developing and international approach to quality assurance and accreditation. There is growing awareness that in the world of cross-border education trade, national quality assurance schemes are becoming challenged by the complexities of the international education environment. While there may be growing awareness, there is no acceptance or agreement that harmonization of national policies with an international approach to quality assessment and accreditation is needed. It is imperative that education specialists discuss and determine the appropriate regulating mechanisms at the national and international level and not leave these questions to the designers and arbitrators of trade agreements. Another, potentially contentious issue is the application of quality assurance schemes to both domestic and foreign providers. It may be that under certain conditions the national treatment obligation requires that all providers, domestic and foreign, be subject to the same processes and criteria. In some countries this will not be a problem, in others it will be fiercely debated. Quality assurance of higher education in some countries is regulated by the sector and in others by the government to a greater or lesser degree. In this area the National Assessment and Accreditation Council (NAAC) is doing a good job. But still lots more have to be done in assessment of the colleges. Recently, the efforts of the NAAC have gathered momentum and hundreds of higher educational institutions are now willing to get assessed and accredited. Against such a backdrop a separate body as exists in Australia for certifying teachers at all levels nationally at regular intervals is required in India to upgrade the education quality. The key point is that authority for quality assurance, regulation and accreditation of cross-border delivery needs to be examined and guided by stakeholders and legitimate bodies related to the education sector and not left solely in the hands of the market.

RESEARCH AND INTELLECTUAL PROPERTY RIGHTS

In the new economy that emphasises knowledge production and trade, there is increasingly more value attributed to the creative and intellectual content inherent in both products and services. The Trade-Related Aspects of Intellectual Property Rights (TRIPs) is another trade agreement, completely separate from the GATS, but which also addresses trade liberalisation. TRIPs cover such things as patents, trademarks and copyright, all of which are salient to the research and teaching/learning functions of higher education. Careful monitoring of TRIPs is also necessary by the higher education sector. A look at the potential implications of trade agreements on research and scholarly work reveals a number of issues. A consistent theme expressed by trade critics is a deep concern about the increased emphasis on commercialization and commodification of the production of knowledge. Skeptics believe that the highly valued trinity of teaching, research and service at traditional universities may be at risk. A more differentiated and niche-oriented approach to higher education may be an unanticipated outcome of increased trade in education and the growing importance of agreements such as GATS and TRIPs.

THE NEGATIVE BALANCE

Balance of trade (trade Surplus) in education is definitely not in our favour for almost a decade. Every year tens of thousands of students leave Indian shores to study abroad. In 2001-02 over 66,000 went to the United States alone—up from 42,000 in 1999-2000 and spending by conservative estimates, over 1.5 billion a year leaving alone UK, Ireland. In addition to this we have to add the franchisee fees charged by the foreign university tag educational shops set-up by flyby private operators and corporate. Now contrast this with the trend of foreign students looking to India for higher education. Addressing a seminar on Internationalisation of Indian Higher

Education—Quality Dimensions in Bangalore, the then Union Minister of State for Human Resource Development, Shri Vallabhai Kathiria, disclosed that the number of foreigners studying in colleges in India had halved over the past decade to a little over 6,000 (This figure has not even reached the figure of students enrolled in Nalanda University of circa 1500). The majority of these were from developing countries poorer than India. If any certificate was required about the quality and image of Indian higher education abroad, surely this statistic says it all. Definitely we have to pull up our higher education from Ice Age to Information Age to face GATS deadline.

In recent years there has been a boost in the number of institutions teaching Indian music, yoga, Sanskrit, Astrology, etc. Some like the Bihar Yoga Bharati in Munger (Bihar) and the Rashtriya Sanskrit Sansthan in Janakpuri (Delhi) today enjoy the same status as deemed universities such as Birla Institute of Technology and Science (BITS), Pilani and Indian Institute of Science (IIS), Bangalore, do. Whether that would attract thousands of foreign students to get a degree in Sanskrit or yoga is another matter all together. The time and market forces will determine the success and failure of our spiritualistic higher education policy.

The number of students in higher education has increased from 200,000 at the time of Independence to 7.5 million today while the number of universities (including deemed universities) has gone from around 20 to more than 300. The crisis in Indian higher education has been known for decades. Obsolete syllabi, lack of multi-disciplinary courses, teacher apathy, excessive examination orientation, poor infrastructure, little research to speak of, bureaucratic meddling, etc. have been identified by a series of education commissions as the ills that plague the system. But precious little has been done over the years and these problems have got worse with the massification of education. Quality problems plaguing Indian higher education can no longer be brushed under the carpet, with India having become a member of the World Trade Organisation in 1994 and a signatory to its General Agreement on Trade in Services (GATS).

Of these, the most threatening for the inertia-ridden Indian higher education establishment is the likelihood of foreign colleges and universities setting up shops in India. With a large English-speaking and affluent middle class, the country is perhaps the most attractive destination in the developing world for overseas education providers. Transnational education shops as mentioned earlier will become a major threat to our education system.

To sum up, the issue is complex and contentious. These two words sum up the current analysis and debate about the impact of GATS on higher education. Opinions on the risks and benefits are divided, if not polarized. They differ within our states and between countries. Each country must undertake the very serious challenge of balancing opportunities and commitments to liberalise trade for exporting higher education services, with the possible impact, related to the same commitments, of the import of education services. This is not an easy task. One can tend to be liberal while considering exporting opportunities and more protectionists when analyzing the implications of importing. At this stage, one is left with the impression that there are more questions than clear answers. Trade in education was alive and well prior to and outside the purview of trade agreements. Yet, it is also critical not to understate the potential implications, risks and opportunities of GATS. Although India has not made any commitment under the GATS agreement, it negotiated in 1994 to allow foreign colleges. The GATS re-negotiations of 2005 made this a possibility. Once India manages to figure out where the water is and where the floor, India can certainly enjoy and benefit from the stay. But the time too short for our faction ridden political and inertia gripped academic establishments and neo-education corporate to speak in one voice.

References

CVCP (2000) The Business of Borderless Education: UK Perspectives, Committees of Vice-Chancellors and Principals, London, United Kingdom.

GATS (1993) General Agreement on Trade in Services, WTO Document, Annex 1-B. http:/www.wto.org/English/does_e/legal_e/final_ehtm#services.

Joshi, M.M. (1998) *Higher Education in India: Vision and Action*. UNESCO World Conference on Higher Education in the Twenty-first Century, Country Paper, October 5-9, Paris.

Kolhatkar, M.R. (1999) *Pre-requisites for Internationalisation of Higher Education.* Paper presented at the Policy Perspective Seminar on Internationalisation of Higher Education, November 26-27, National Institute of Educational Planning and Administration, New Delhi.

Knight, Jane (1999) A Time of Turbulence and Transformation for Internationalisation, Research Monograph 14, Canadian Bureau for International Education, Ottawa, Canada.

Power, K.B. (2002) Indian Higher Education—A Conglomerate of Concepts, Facts and Practices, New Delhi : Concept Publishing House.

WTO (1999) The WTO in Brief, Prepared by the WTO Secretariat, Geneva, Switzerland, ww/v./yto.org/English/thewto_e/whails_e/whatis_e.htm

WTO (1999) The general Agreement in Trade in Services_objectives, coverage and discipline, Prepared by the WTO Secretariat, www.wto.org/english/tratop_e/serv_e/gatsqa_e.htm

WTO. (1999) The Services Sectoral Classification List, World Trade Organisation. Prepared by WTO.

14

Is Educational Financing in India Adequate?

L.N. Dash

Education has played a role in economic thought. The Classical economists accepted education as means to increase production. Adam Smith deemed acquisition of skills through education and study (Vaizey, 1968). David Ricardo and Thomas Malthus considered education as means to develop habits that would be helpful to check population growth. Alfred Marshall in his *Principles of Economics* refers education as a national investment. (Vaizey, 1968) Marshall viewed that the most valuable of all capital is that invested in human beings. According to him the direct returns are higher through the development of 'genius'. There was growing interest in the economic value of education during the 1960s which has been rightly termed by Bowman as the "human investment revolution in economic thought." (1966) During the early 1960s, economists like Schultz (1963), Denison (1962 and 1967), and Kruger (1968) highlighted the contribution of education to economic growth. Gary S. Becker (1975) examined the concept of investment in human capital. According to Galbraith the role of education is paramount in the social and economic development of a country (Prasad, 2000). Education not only improves the productivity of labour but also permits greater specialization, said Eckaus (1968).

EDUCATION AND ECONOMIC DEVELOPMENT

Education is generally regarded as a public good and as a merit good which produces a variety of externalities (Tilak, 1995). Contribution of education to economic growth, distribution, and reduction in fertility rates, etc. are the different ways in which education generates public good. Some of the non-economic benefits of education are better citizenry, reduction in crime, improved health conditions, and political democracy which are also important for accelerating the economic development of a country. Investment in education contributes to the economic development of a country in very many ways. There is a strong relationship between education and economic growth. That education contributes to economic growth in a great way has been revealed by the study of McClelland (1966). Harbison and Myer's study of 75 nations shows the correlation between GNP per capita and school enrolment (1964). Denison and others have calculated that the contribution of education in the United States was accounted for due to increased education of the labour force. Bowman and Anderson (1963), Kaser (1966) and others have also found correlation between level of per capita income and level of educational development. Wheeler (1980) has depicted that an increase in literacy rate from 20 to 30 per cent gives rise to an increase of GDP by 8 to 16 per cent. Marris (1982) examined data for 66 developing countries in a similar way and concluded that education influences economic growth in a strong way. Education also makes indirect contribution to economic growth in a number of ways. For example, Easterlin examined the relationship between education and economic growth in twenty-five of the largest countries of the world and found that the spread of technology in these countries could be possible because of the development of formal schooling (1981).

Cochrane has pointed out that education has important links with other aspects of human resource development such as health and fertility (1979). Improvement in education can help alleviate poverty both directly and indirectly by increasing income and reducing family size. There is a better chance that the educated parents will have healthy and well-nourished children. The study of Noor has concluded that there is a relationship between education and other forms of social development (1981). The findings of the study of Colclough strengthens the view point that primary schooling has positive effects on various aspects of social policy issues like family size, health, nutrition, demography, rural development, etc. (1980). The strong link between education and life expectancy, disease and nutrition has been reinforced by Cochrane, O'Hara and Leslie (1980). Their analysis strengthened the point that the rate of reduction of mortality in the developing countries has slowed down because of the progress of education. The link between fertility and children's education has been explained by Gary S. Becker with the help of the 'quantity-quality trade-off' model (1981). According to Becker, child schooling is an investment in human capital which raises child quality which ultimately reduces demand for quantity. Another important indirect effect of education is that it raises the productivity of farmers (Jamison and Lau, 1982). Studies in Korea, Malaysia, Nepal and Thailand show that education raises the physical productivity of farmers. Four years of schooling for farmers, on an average, appears to increase the output of farmers by about eight per cent. The farmers in Thailand are more likely to use chemical inputs, improved seeds, and irrigation if they had primary education (Jamison and Lau, 1982).

A number of studies in India also show that education has contributed a great deal to India's economic development in all its facets. Loh's study of 14 most populated states in India during the period 1961-81 reveals that one additional year of education of the workforce was associated with a 15 per cent increase in economic output (Loh, 1995). Mathur's analysis of 306 districts of India laid bare the fact that there is a great correlation between human capital and India's development (1993). He concludes that although higher levels of education have great bearing on economic development, primary and middle schooling are no less important as they create conditions conducive to economic development. The link between human capital and economic development is stronger at higher levels of education. The level of education development also influences poverty reduction as well as economic growth. Higher literacy level is one of the factors responsible poverty reduction (Datt and Ravallion, 1995). The 1987-88 National Sample Survey (NSS) results show that the relation between poverty and educational attainment is very strong in Maharashtra. It has been found in the high productivity areas in Punjab, Haryana and Uttar Pradesh that general education up to secondary level has a significant effect on diffusion of technology and agricultural productivity of cultivators. Nautiyal's analysis in Uttar Pradesh has established the high correlations between educational levels, improved farm practices and high crop yielding of important crops (1989).

Apart from the direct benefits of education, there are a number of indirect benefits of education for India's development. Schooling has strongly influenced decrease in fertility rate all the world over. In India too the fertility pattern is in line with the international pattern. The total fertility rate falls with increase in education. The National Family Health Survey (NFHS) 1992-93 confirms strong effect of primary education on fertility rate. In a study conducted by A.M. Basu it is revealed that among urban women 28 per cent of those with some education had ever used contraceptive methods compared with 8 per cent of those with no education (1992). In northern India mothers with secondary education experienced 77 per thousand few deaths among sons under age 5 and 96 per thousand few deaths among daughters under 5 as compared to non-literate mothers (World Bank, 1997). In the urban areas there were 82 per thousand child mortality for mothers with no schooling areas and 34 per thousand for those with some schooling. In addition to this schooling improves a mother's basic child care skills, efforts at preventive care, and use of modern medical services. This has been concluded by Dasgupta from her study in Punjab. Mothers' education also influences children's nutritional status. The two-village study indicates that in West Bengal children of literate mothers had higher nutritional intakes than children of non-literate mothers (Sen and Sengupta, 1983). The NFHS reports that in Uttar Pradesh and Tamil Nadu the likelihood that a child will be severely undernourished declines with increase in mothers' educational level.

All these confirm the view that the economic and social benefits of education are highest where there is a minimum level of education among all sections of the society. Despite this India has not fared well in this field. The literacy rate stood at 65.38 per cent in 2001 which is less than many developing countries. There are also sex differentials in literacy as only 54.16 per cent of the female population was literate as against 75.85 for males. There are also wide differences between the states and within the same states. For example, Kerala has the highest literacy rate of 90.92 per cent while Bihar and Rajasthan have literacy rates of 47.5 per cent and 61 per cent respectively. Moreover, the SC and ST population, women, rural people, and the poorer sections of the society—all have literacy rates that are lower than the national average. Females make up labour 60 per cent of the non-literate in India. Despite the improvement in scholl enrolment, 95 lakh children were out of school in 2005. About one-third of the entrants at the primary level are females notwithstanding the fact that primary education is very important in India for integration with the world economy. However, for completing primary education, the target of the UN Millennium Development Goals (MDGs) as well as India's Sarva Siksha Abhiyan (education for all) is not enough. Many of those who complete schools cannot read simple texts nor do simple sums. A functionally illiterate society is the biggest impediment for economic development. Spending on education, therefore, is not simply consumption but it is an investment in human capital. Investing on education is highly rewarding both to society and to the individual as well. Therefore, an attempt is made to find out the size of education financing in India over time and space.

EDUCATIONAL FINANCING IN INDIA

Availability of financial resources is vital for formulating policies and implementing programmes and projects which in turn help in the expansion of education. The National Policy on

Education of India set the goal of educational expenditure at 6 per cent of the GDP. As against this, the combined total expenditure on education by the Central and the State governments was 3.49 per cent of GDP in 2004-05 (Government of India, 2006). The average government spending of the top 100 countries of the world is 5.24 per cent, which is about 50 per cent more than India's. China spends 8 per cent of the GDP on education. The Government of India's central plan allocation for education has reached a staggering height of Rs. 15,244 crore in 2005-06. The allocation for different types of education is like this: Rs. 290 crore for adult education and Rs. 2712 crore for secondary education. Allocation for elementary education in the Tenth Five-Year Plan (2002-07) is Rs. 28,750 crore which is 75 per cent higher than the allocation in the Ninth Plan. Resources for elementary education have been augmented through imposition of the two per cent education cess. Because of the imposition of the education cess, budgeted outlay for elementary and adult education more than doubled from Rs. 6,000 crore in 2004-05 to Rs. 12,532 crore in 2005-06 (Table 14.1).

The exponential growth in the number of private technical colleges, increased commercialization of technical-engineering, management education and lack of any significant presence in among the top institutes across the world has worried the government. To take corrective measures, the government has chalked out an investment plan for the sectors. In 2005-06, Rs. 17,760 crore had been allocated to the technical education. The government has plans to increase the allocation in this sector in future. Out of the one crore students enrolled in higher education about 20 lakh were in technical education. However, technical education accounts for only 0.4 per cent of total government expenditure. As with higher education, lack of investment across the technical education sector has meant lack of access, equity and quality. The government now wants to ensure larger allocation for this sector. The government increased allocation for institutions like Indian School of Mines, Dhanbad, National Institute of Industrial Engineering, National Institute of Foundry and Forge Technology, and School of Planning and Architecture, from Rs. 19 crore to Rs. 29 crore in 2006-07. It is also going to set-up a school of medicine and bio-sciences at IIT, Kharagpur, which would mean allocation of

TABLE 14.1
Plan Expenditure on Different Sectors of Education

(in per cent)

Sector	*First Plan*	*Second Plan*	*Third Plan*	*Fourth Plan*	*Fifth Plan*	*Sixth Plan*	*Seventh Plan*	*Eighth Plan*	*Ninth Plan*	*Tenth Plan*
(1)	*(2)*	*(3)*	*(4)*	*(5)*	*(6)*	*(7)*	*(8)*	*(9)*	*(10)*	*(11)*
Elementary education	58 (870)	35 (950)	34 (2010)	50 (8414)	52 (5913)	32 (8414)	37 (28494)	48 (103940)	65.7 (145233)	65.6 (287500)
Secondary education	5 (80)	19 (510)	18 (1030)			20 (5344)	24 (18315)	24 (52311)	10.5 (23227)	9.9 (43250)
Adult education				2 (126)	2 (248)	6 (1535)	6 (4696)	5 (11421)	24 (5204)	2.9 (12500)
Higher education	8 (120)	18 (480)	15 (870)	25 (1883)	28 (3188)	21 (5604)	16 (12011)	10 (20944)	10.3 (22709)	9.5 (41765)
Others	15 (230)	10(300)	12(730)	13 (936)	9(1071)	11(2729)	3(1980)	3(7398)	1.6(3492)	1.4(6235)
Technical education	14 (210)	18 (490)	21 (1250)	10 (786)	9 (1015)	10 (2563)	14 (10833)	10 (21987)	9.5 (21095)	10.7 (47000)
Total	100 (1510)	100 (2730)	100 (5890)	100 (7474)	100 (11435)	100 (26187)	100 (76329)	100 (218001)	100 (220960)	100 (438250)

Source : Gopalji and Suman Bhakri, *Statistical Data on Indian Economy* (New Delhi: Taxmann Allied Services, 2005), p. 18.

Rs. 20 crore. Another Rs. 42 crore has been spent for upgrading of seven engineering institutes identified by the S.K. Joshi Committee to the level of IITs. It proposes Rs. 130 crore allocations for the Indian Institute of Science of Bangalore. The government has a proposal to spend about Rs. 100 crore for the newly-established Indian Institute of Science Education and Research (IISER) at Pune and Kolkata, which will commence with the academic session 2006-07. An amount of Rs. 25 crore is earmarked for the Indian Institutes of Information Technology, Design and Manufacturing at Jabalpur and Kancheepuram. The HRD Ministry has the plan to set-up 20 Indian Institutes of Information Technology (IIITs) in the Eleventh Plan (2007-12), four in each year of the plan period, in 20 states. Such a step has been taken keeping in view the finding of the Nasscom-Mckinsey Report, 2005. The report has said that India would need a 2.3 million strong BPO workforce by 2010 to maintain its current market share. It is expected that the IT sector will grow at a rate of 25 per cent and achieve a level of $ 60 billion by 2010. The scheme of IIITs in 20 states would need Rs. 3700 crore over a period of six years. Of this, an amount of Rs. 2500 crore is earmarked for plan expenditure and Rs. 1200 crore for non-plan expenditure.

The Central government, state governments, and households are the main sources of finance for education. The ability of the state governments to finance education depends on their revenue raising ability, the transfer of resources through the finance and Planning Commission. Household spending on education reflects the levels and distribution of income. As total expenditure on education is low, expenditure by the Central and state governments was only 3.5 per cent of GDP which rose to 4.3 and 4.4 per cent in 1999-2000 and 2000-01 respectively. Thereafter, it again plummeted to 3.81 per cent in 2003-04 and 3.54 in 2004-05. On the contrary, state expenditure as a share of GDP is below the desired level. The share of total budgetary resources devoted to education in India has been increasing, from 7.92 per cent in 1951-52 to 12.54 per cent in 2002-03. However, it is still below the average of 17.5 per cent for all low-income countries excluding India and China.

Education's share in states' total budgetary allocation declines. Twenty-nine major states together have allocated just about 7.2 per cent of their aggregate budgetary expenses on education in 2005-06. This was 10.2 percentage points lower than what they allocated five years ago in 2000-01 (Table 14.3). In actual terms, budgetary allocation under this head has increased by an annual compound rate of 6.7 per cent as compared to a huge 27.2 per cent annual rise in states' aggregate expenditure during the same period. In 2005-06 the allocation under expenditure increased by 8.5 per cent over the previous year compared to 16 per cent rise in 2004-05. This was the picture of the country as a whole. At the individual level, many states did even worse. In Punjab, for example, education accounted for a paltry 4 per cent in total budgetary expenses of the state in 2005-06 (Table 14.2). Education's share was 4.2 per cent in Madhya Pradesh and 4.5 per cent in Gujarat during the same period—substantially lower than the national average. In fact, the share of education in total budgetary allocation was lower than the national average in as many as 12 of the 29 states in 2005-06. Most of these states have witnessed a decline in the share of education in their total budgetary allocation during the last five years (Table 14.3). Among the major states, Kerala has witnessed the sharpest decline of 13.3 percentage points from 20.1 per cent in 2000-01 to 6.8 per cent in 2005-06. At 6.8 per cent the share of education in total budgetary allocation in Kerala was lower than that of the national average. This is surprising considering the state's record in literacy drive. Maharashtra has witnessed the second biggest decline—the share of education in the state's total budgetary allocation has declined by a massive 13.2 percentage points from 22.3 per cent in 2000-01 to 9.1 per cent in 2005-06. Education's share in total budgetary allocation has fallen by 12.5 percentage points in Uttaranchal, 12.4 percentage points in Rajasthan and 12.2 percentage points in Madhya Pradesh. But what is more disturbing is that the actual allocation for education in Maharastra has declined, albeit marginally, in 2005-06 over 2004-05—down by 0.1 per cent from Rs. 10,239 crore in 2004-05 to Rs. 10,226 crore in 2005-06 (Table 14.3). Arunachal Pradesh, Manipur and Mizoram are the three other states which too have witnessed a decline in actual allocation under this head during this period (Table 14.2).

TABLE 14.2
Expenditure on Education

(*Rs. in Crore*)

State	*2005-06*	*2004-05*	*2003-04*	*2002-03*	*2001-02*	*2000-01*
(1)	(2)	(3)	(4)	(5)	(6)	(7)
Andhra Pradesh	5879.19	5384.45	4667.84	4027.18	3871.04	3740.30
Arunachal Pradesh	195.58	219.76	198.66	165.58	183.20	77.24
Assam	3553.58	3198.35	2363.78	1998.02	1872.49	1943.52
Bihar	4485.57	4143.86	3607.36	3259.98	3076.22	4012.27
Chhattisgarh	1417.29	1304.46	969.45	750.47	696.59	250.32
Goa	374.61	362.36	292.34	286.32	247.25	233.13
Gujarat	4117.03	4093.72	3692.64	3634.36	3263.55	3684.77
Haryana	2099.60	1793.49	1540.68	1455.01	1479.66	1334.47
Himachal Pradesh	1085.36	1072.20	1005.61	957.34	918.72	904.52
Jammu & Kashmir	1276.09	1080.67	977.50	955.59	936.70	866.84
Jharkhand	2104.13	1739.23	1379.37	1859.34	1283.06	—
Karnataka	4889.50	4505.33	3771.34	3570.72	3505.88	3488.75
Kerala	3884.24	3645.83	3094.80	2986.22	2489.81	2635.52
Madhya Pradesh	2873.79	2720.61	2375.77	2312.14	2125.86	2762.53
Maharashtra	10,226.90	10,238.58	9440.98	8941.40	9387.91	9420.25

Manipur	381.90	415.39	304.94	286.25	290.60	279.51
Meghalaya	402.28	346.73	269.06	242.30	250.08	236.86
Mizoram	237.87	257.91	218.36	204.26	213.89	189.86
Nagaland	292.55	284.30	256.41	210.05	223.01	237.68
Orissa	2178.43	1967.84	1899.52	1902.44	1755.64	1760.48
Punjab	2643.02	2493.02	2080.81	2092.76	1832.93	1859.24
Rajasthan	5043. 60	4093.33	3655.09	3329.86	3455.52	3286.28
Sikkim	223.18	210.23	174.15	161.19	152.44	134.09
Tamil Nadu	5283.89	4642.74	4254.13	4158.92	4299.80	4409.67
Tripura	617.73	553.57	504.47	485.23	459.25	411.40
Uttaranchal	1401.17	1329.99	1094.04	969.31	696.92	238.63
Uttar Pradesh	8707.38	7679.18	6315.77	6137.29	6088.10	6172.52
West Bengal	5594.45	5246.41	4522.60	4405.72	4552.45	4581.63
Delhi	1816.74	1766.93	1271.74	1237.53	1184.53	1115.02
All States	83,286.65	76,790.47	66,191.21	62,982.78	60,793.10	60,267.30

Source : RBI, *State Finances—A Study of Budgets* (Various Issues).

Table 14.3
Share of Education in State's Total Expenditure

(in per cent)

State	*2005-06*	*2004-05*	*2003-04*	*2002-03*	*2001-02*	*2000-01*
Andhra Pradesh	8.5	8.7	3.4	11.7	12.5	13.3
Arunachal Pradesh	5.0	5.7	2.6	12.1	13.3	6.4
Assam	15.6	10.0	11.4	22.4	21.9	25.5
Bihar	14.2	13.9	13.8	18.4	20.7	23.7
Chhattisgarh	4.8	4.5	3.1	11.0	12.4	13.1
Goa	6.7	7.7	4.4	11.9	10.5	11.9
Gujarat	4.5	4.1	5.2	13.5	12.7	13.6
Haryana	7.3	6.3	4.7	13.7	13.8	14.6
Himachal Pradesh	11.5	11.6	6.1	14.5	16.2	17.0
Jammu & Kashmir	9.3	8.9	8.9	10.9	11.6	11.1
Jharkhand	13.5	11.7	11.3	19.0	16.2	—
Karnataka	9.5	9.0	5.2	14.8	16.0	17.7
Kerala	6.8	6.3	5.8	17.6	19.0	20.1
Madhya Pradesh	4.2	3.9	4.2	12.2	12.5	16.3
Maharashtra	9.1	7.0	9.3	18.9	22.1	22.3
Manipur	8.6	9.5	7.5	13.3	13.7	20.2
Meghalaya	2.7	2.4	2.1	15.3	17.9	16.6
Mizoram	13.2	11.5	5.7	14.5	16.0	14.7
Nagaland	8.1	8.2	3.8	11.0	11.0	12.9
Orissa	8.2	6.5	6.0	14.3	14.6	15.9
Punjab	4.0	3.8	3.3	12.1	11.7	13.2
Rajasthan	6.4	5.1	4.9	15.5	18.2	18.8
Sikkim	6.0	5.1	5.6	7.6	8.0	14.2
Tamil Nadu	6.0	4.4	4.8	13.7	17.3	18.0
Tripura	8.4	8.0	7.3	19.1	18.6	19.3
Uttaranchal	9.0	9.2	3.6	20.0	21.1	21.5
Uttar Pradesh	8.0	6.5	2.9	14.6	16.0	16.8
West Bengal	5.0	4.6	3.7	15.9	16.2	17.1
Delhi	15.8	12.8	10.9	12.1	13.7	15.1
All States	7.2	6.2	5.0	15.0	16.1	17.4

Source : RBI, *State Finances—A Study of Budgets* (Various Issues).

TABLE 14.4
Public Expenditure on Education in India

(in crore)

Year	*Government expenditure on education (centre + state)*	*Total Government expenditure on all sectors*	*GDP at current prices (at factor cost) base year 1993-94*	*% of expenditure on education to expenditure on all sectors*	*% of education expenditure to GDP*
1951-52	64.46	814.13	10,080	7.92	0.64
1955-56	118.39	1,111.26	10,332	10.65	1.15
1960-61	239.56	1,997.93	16,220	11.99	1.48
1965-66	432.61	4,404.82	25,586	9.82	1.69
1970-71	892.36	8,787.12	42,222	1016	2.11
1975-76	1,849.47	17,958.99	75,709	10.30	2.44
1980-81	3,884.20	36,398.39	1,30,178	10.67	2.98
1985-86	8,713.02	67,091.41	2,49,547	12.99	3.49
1990-91	19,615.85	1,46,711.53	5,10,954	13.37	3.84
1995-96	38,178.09	2,86,194.55	10,73,271	13.34	3.56
1996-97	43,896.48	3,29,389.92	12,43,546	13.33	3.53
1997-98	48,552.14	3,80,728.45	13,90,148	12.75	3.49
1998-99	61,578.91	4,39,768.11	15,98,127	14.00	3.85
1999-2000	74,816.09	5,12,519.33	17,61,838	14.60	4.25
2000-01	82,486.43	5,72,160.14	19,02,998	14.42	4.33
2001-02	79,865.70	6,19,713.14	20,90,957	12.89	3.82
2002-03	89,220.45	7,00,389.87	22,49,493	12.74	3.97

Source : Government of India, Ministry of Human Resource Development, *Selected Educational Statistics, 2002-03* (New Delhi: Government of India, 2004), pp. 3-4.

Plan expenditure on different sectors of education indicates that elementary education received greater emphasis since the Ninth Plan period. During the Ninth Plan 65.7 per cent of total plan expenditure of Rs. 220,960 crore on education was spent on elementary education. The percentage allocation for this remained almost the same at 65.6 per cent during the Tenth Plan period. The expenditure trend on elementary education shows that the figure has soared from Rs. 870 crore in the First Five-Year Plan to Rs. 287,500 crore in the Tenth Plan period (Table 14.1). Similarly, expenditure on secondary education in India has escalated from Rs. 80 crore in the First Plan to Rs. 43,250 crore in the Tenth Plan. In percentage terms there have been fluctuations in expenditure on secondary education over the planning era; but perceptible increase is not noticed. However, during the Ninth and Tenth Plan periods, the total allocation for this sector stood at Rs. 23,227 and Rs. 432,250 crore (Table 14.1). Spending on adult education began from Fourth Plan period and 2.9 per cent of the total allocation for education during the Tenth Plan went for this sub-sector. Higher and technical education received Rs. 41,765 crore (9.5 per cent) and Rs. 47,000 crore (10.7 per cent) respectively during the Tenth Plan. The entire spectrum of public expenditure on education shows that while expenditure on education is increasing of late, elementary education receives top priority.

The pattern of household expenditure on education as has been estimated by the 52 round of NSSO (2002) shows that states like Uttar Pradesh, West Bengal, Tamil Nadu, Maharashtra, and Andhra Pradesh spend more on education in absolute terms. For example, Uttar Pradesh spends Rs. 4140 crore, West Bengal's 3496 crore, etc. The household expenditure on education of all the states and Union Territories stand at Rs. 30,810 crore which is 38.58 per cent of the government expenditure on education. In percentage terms, the household expenditure in Haryana is 77 per cent, Punjab 69 per cent, Tamil Nadu 53 per cent, Kerala 54 per cent, Gujarat 53 per cent, etc. On the other side there are states like Orissa (23.89 per cent), Assam (25.40 per cent), Chhattisgarh (31.36 per cent), Himachal Pradesh (27.02 per cent), and Rajasthan (31.08 per cent) where households spend less as a percentage of government expenditure.

CONCLUSION

India, in order to become a knowledge economy, has to develop its human capital base. A transition to the knowledge economy can be made only if more funds are allocated to the education sector. Further, the per student expenditure pattern for primary, secondary and tertiary education shows that the expenditure composition is skewed towards secondary and tertiary education. At the primary level, public expenditure per student is $ 7.2 which increases to $ 23.01 and $ 92.5 at the secondary and tertiary levels. The pattern is completely different in case of South Korea. Per student public expenditure goes on diminishing from $ 14 at the primary level to $ 17.9 and $ 7.37 at the secondary and tertiary levels respectively. Tertiary education, of course, is expensive. Keeping in view the GDP level of India, more private investment should be encouraged in the higher education level and more public investment should be made for primary and secondary education. This will help to strengthen the human capital resource base and need of the knowledge economy.

References

Basu, A.M. (1992) *Culture: The Status of Women and Demographic Behaviour,* Oxford, Clarendon.

Becker, Gary S. (1975) *Human Capital: A Theoretical and Empirical Analysis, With Special Refernce to Education,* New York, National Bureau of Economic Research.

Becker, Gary S. (1981) *A Treatise on the Family,* Cambridge, Mass, Harvard University Press.

Bowman, M.J. and Anderson. (1963) "Connecting the Role of Education in Development", in C. Geertz (ed.), *Old Societies and New States,* Glencoe, Ill., Free Press.

Brown, M.J. (1966) "The Human Investment Revolution in Economic Thought", *Sociology of Education,* Spring, pp. 111-37.

Cochrane, Susan H. (1979) *Fertility and Education: What Do We Really Know?* Baltimore: John Hopkins University Press.

Cochrane, Susan H. and Farid, Samir (1984) *Fertility in Sub-Saharan Africa: Levels and Their Explanation,* Washington, D.C., World Bank.

Cochrane, Susan H. O'Hara, Donald. and Leslie, Joane (1980) *The Effects of Education on Health,* World Bank Staff Working Paper No. 405, Washington, D.C., World Bank.

Colclough, Christopher. (1980) *Primary Schooling and Economic Development,* World Bank Staff Working Paper No. 399, London, John Wiley.

Curle, A. (1964) "Education, Politics and Development", *Comparative Education Review,* Vol. VII, No. 3, pp. 226-45.

Dasgupta, Monika "Death Clustering, Mothers' Education, and the Determinants of Child Mortality in Rural Punjab, India", *Population Studies*, 44, pp. 489-505.

Datt, Gaurav and Ravallion, Martin (1995) *Why Some Indian States Have Done Better Than Others at Raising Rural Living Standards*, Washington, D.C., World Bank.

Denison, E.F. (1962) *The Sources of Economic Growth in the United States and the Alternative Before Us*, New York, Committee for Economic Development.

Denison, E.F. (1967) *Why Growth Rates Differ: Post-War Experience in Nine Western Countries*, Washington, D.C., Brookings Institution.

Easterlin, R. (1981) "Why is not the Whole Developed?" *Journal of Economic History*, 41, March, pp. 1-19.

Eckaus, Richard S. "Education and Economic Growth", in UNESCO, *Readings in the Economics of Education*, Paris, UNESCO, pp. 571-73.

Government of India (2006) *Economic Survey, 2005-06*, New Delhi, Government of India.

Harbison, F. and Myres, C.A. (1964) *Education, Manpower, and Economic Growth*, New York, McGraw-Hill.

Jamison, David T. and Lau, Laurence, J. (1982) *Farmer Education and Farm Efficiency*, Baltimore, John Hopkins University Press.

Kasker, M. (1966) "Education and Economic Progress: Experience in Industrialised Market Economies", in E.A.G Robinson and J. Vaizey (eds.), *The Economics of Education* , New York, St. Martin Press.

Kruger, A.O. (1968) "Factor Endowment and per Capita Income Differences among Countries", *Economic Journal*, Sept., Vol. 78, pp. 641-59.

Loh, Jacqueline (1995) "Education and Economic Growth in India: An Aggregate Production Function Approach", New Delhi, Ministry of Human Resource Development.

Marhur, Ashok (1993) "The Human Capital Stock and Regional Economic Development", in S.C. Nana (ed.), *Regional Disparities in Educational Development*, New Delhi, South Asian Publishers.

Marris, R. (1982) *Economic Growth in Cross Section*, London, Birkbeck College, Department of Economics.

McClelland, David (1966) "Does Education Accelerate Economic Growth", *Economic Development and Cultural Change*, Vol. XIV, No. 3, April, pp. 257-78.

Nautiyal, K.C. (1989) *Education and Rural Poor*, New Delhi, Commonwealth.

Noor, Abdum (1981) *Education and Basic Human Needs*, World Bank Staff Working Paper No. 450, Washington, D.C., World Bank.

Prasad, Narendra (2000) "Economics of Education: The Real Issue of Indian Economic Development in 21st Century", in B.N. Singh, M.P. Shrivastava and N. Prasad, *Indian Economy in the Twenty-first Century*, New Delhi, Anmol Publications.

Schultz, T.W. (1961) "Education and Economic Growth", in N.B. Henry (ed.), *Social Forces Influencing American Education*, Chicago, National Society for the Study in Education, University of Chicago Press.

Schultz, T.W. (1963) *The Economic Value of Education,* New York, Columbia University Press.

Sen, Amartya and Sengupta, Sunil (1983) "Malnutrition of Rural Children and the Sex Bias", *Economic and Political Weekly,* 19, (Annual issue).

Tilak, Jandhyala B.G. (1995) 'Cost Recovery Approaches in Education in India,' Occasional Papers, New Delhi, NIEPA

Vaizey, John (1968) "What Some Economists Said about Education?" in UNESCO, *Readings in the Economics of Education,* Paris, UNESCO.

Wheeler, D. (1980) *Human Resource Development and Economic Growth in Developing Countries,* World Bank Staff Working Paper No. 407, Washington, D.C., World Bank.

World Bank (1995) *Advancing Social Development,* Washington D.C., World Bank.

World Bank (1997) *Primary Education in India,* Washington D.C., World Bank.

15

Public Expenditure on Higher Education in India

SHAIKH SALEEM AND VIDYA GAWAL

INTRODUCTION

In order to meet the challenges of the 21st century and to acquire a competitive edge, the higher education system of India has to transform to make it more socially relevant, technology-oriented, diversified and of high quality. The skills and specialization of graduates produced by our system should match the real needs of the productive sectors in the market place and the changing needs of our society. But the main issues concerning higher education in India is financial stress. The various sources of finance for higher education in India are like government sector (central government, and state government) and non-governmental sector (students/parents or families, corporate) are not able to meet the financial requirements.

However, it should be noted that the Government has made huge investments in higher education in independent

India. But the rate of investment is not able to cope up with the increasing needs stemming from population growth. Currently India is spending 4.1 per cent of GDP on education and out of which just 1 per cent of GDP on higher education, is too small for the country like India having population of 108 crore. The expenditure on education by the government is not sufficient especially on higher education.

With reference to primary education , the Central Advisory Board for Education (CABE) calculated that the implementation of the Education Bill would have required an additional amount of Rs. 53,500-72,700 crore a year over a six year period in addition to the Rs. 47,100 crore that was spent on elementary education in 2003-04. This would mean an estimated increase of 6.4 to 8.5 per cent to the Central Government's annual budget. Considering that an education Cess of Rs. 5010 crore was collected in 2004-05, and that only Rs. 2000 crore was spend for that purpose, and again considering that the government has given a corporate subsidy of Rs. 90,000 crore through the SEZ bill is evident where the priority lies. This shows that the Government is ignoring the important sector and rather investing in sectors, which are likely to yield dividends.

THE GOVERNMENT SHARE IN HIGHER EDUCATION

The government share in higher education has not increased significantly in recent years. This is primarily because of the mounting debts rather than ideological overtones, as India already has a debt of US $136.5 billion up to September 2006 (*www.finmin.ac.in website of Finance ministry of India*). Public Expenditure on higher education was 0.75 per cent of GDP in 1991-92 which has not even doubled after 15 year. In 2005-06 government spending is less than one per cent of the GDP on higher education.

Although public expenditure on higher education has been augmented to Rs. 2712 crore, and on technical education to Rs. 733.40 crore for 2005-06 (about one per cent of the GDP), it is not sufficient in terms of unit cost per student (Budget Analysis, 2005-06). Since 2003, the Government of India introduced 2 per cent cess, a special tax on all trading just to generate additional resources for education, but this amount cannot be used for higher education. It is earmarked solely for primary education, which is a constitutional obligation for all governments in India. Demand for higher educated manpower will increase substantially in the near future and this will impel central focus on the quality and quantity of manpower produced by the higher education system. Both for quantitative expansion and improvement in quality, the system requires large additional resources. Table 15.1 depicts the public expenditure on higher education. The figure shows that the current public expenditure is not sufficient to achieve the desired goals of higher education.

TABLE 15.1
Public Expenditure on Higher Education in India

Year	*Expenditure on education in terms of % of GDP*	*Expenditure on higher education in terms of % of total expenditure on education*	*Expenditure on higher education in terms of % of GDP*
1990-91	3.84	20.05	0.77
1991-92	3.80	19.73	0.75
1992-93	3.72	19.62	0.73
1993-94	3.62	19.61	0.71
1994-95	3.56	19.38	0.69
1995-96	3.56	18.25	0.65
1996-97	3.53	18.13	0.64
1997-98	3.49	17.76	0.62
1998-99	3.85	17.92	0.69
1999-2000	4.25	20.23	0.86
2000-01	4.33	20.55	0.89
2001-02	3.82	18.06	0.69
2002-03	3.80	18.42	0.7
2003-04	3.76	18.08	0.68

Source : Department of Higher Education, Ministry of Human Resource Development, Government of India (*website: www. education.nic.in*).

INTERNATIONAL COMPARISON IN EXPENDITURE ON HIGHER EDUCATION

India is being projected as a would-be super-power by the year 2020. Some time this projection seems to be baseless if we look the literacy rate of India and growth of the educational sector. The overall literacy rate as per the census 2001 is 64.8 per cent which is very less as compared to the developed nations like US, Japan, China and Russia, etc. At present there are 300 million adult illiterates in India and only 60 million out of 170 million children at the primary school level are able to make to secondary education. Out of these 160 million, only 9 million make it to post-secondary education. Especially India is far behind in development of higher educational system. May be because of expenditure on higher education is small compared to other developed countries. India spends just $ 406 (about Rs. 18,600) per student on higher education. That is just a fraction of the spending by countries like China ($ 2,728 or Rs. 125,000), Brazil ($ 3,986 or Rs. 182,000) and Malaysia ($ 11,790 or Rs. 540,000).

The public expenditure of countries like U.S and Japan are almost 1.4 per cent and 0.5 per cent of GDP on higher education. In absolute terms the current GDP of US is $ 11,667 billion and Japan $ 4,623 billion which far outweigh the expenditure by India. (UNDP & Word Bank reports 2005 and 2006). Thus the statistics show that if India spends on par with the developed nations in terms of the percentage of GDP, still the expenditure by India on education will be less as its total GDP size much less than the developed countries. Table 15.2 depicts the international comparison in higher education. Just 65 per cent of the population of India is literate; the literacy level of the other developed nations is either 100 per cent or almost nearing 100 per cent. For instance, the literacy in the U.S is 99 per cent and in the U.K it is 99 per cent. Yet they are spending larger amount on education compared to India. All this show that India should double its the current public expenditure on education to achieve the 100 per cent literacy level.

TABLE 15.2
International Comparisons in Higher Education

Country	*Literacy (% of population)*	*GDP (in $ billion)*	*Expenditure on education in terms of % of GDP (2000-02)*	*Expenditure on higher education in terms of % of GDP*
France	99	2,002	5.6	1
Canada	99	979	5.2	1.8
U.S.	99	11,667	5.1	1.4
U.K.	99	2,140	4.7	1.1
Germany	99	2,714	4.3	1.1
India	65	691	4.1	0.8
Japan	99	4,623	3.9	0.5

Source : UNDP, *Human Development Report 2005* and World Bank Report 2005 and 2006.

NEED TO INCREASE PUBLIC EXPENDITURE ON HIGHER EDUCATION

Currently mere 9.8 million students are admitted into the country's 15,800 colleges and 380 universities *(Annual Status of Education Report 2005)*. It may however be pointed out that while India has the second largest system of higher education, next only to the U.S., the student enrolment ratio in higher education is just 7.2 per cent. However, this rate is very low in comparison to other developed nations. The enrolment ratio in higher education is 80 per cent in USA, 50 per cent in France, 30 per cent in UK, 13 per cent in China, even in developing and less developed nations the enrolment ratio is higher than in India. One of the reasons may be that the present number of universities, colleges, resources and facilities are insufficient to cope up with the growing demands for higher education. The figure shows that the number of universities and colleges are small compared to other nations. Table 15.3 depicts the comparison of population and number of universities. To compete successfully in the knowledge-based economy of the 21st Century, India needs enough universities, colleges and required resources and facilities. Under this circumstances the government should take a new look at sources of funding for higher education.

Table 15.3
Population and Number of Universities in Selected Countries

Country	*Population (Million)*	*No. of Universities*
USA	295	2364
UK	59	104
Japan	127	684
Germany	82	330
India	1105	380

Source : CIA World Fact Book (website: www.nationmaster.com).

SUGGESTIONS

Faced with financial crises coupled with competing demands for funds for different sectors of the economy, the state and Central Governments have not been able to allocate adequate resources for higher education. We are far behind the target of spending 6 per cent of the GNP on education as recommended by the Education Commission (1964-66), and in the recent years the relative share of higher education in the allocation of funds has also declined, primarily due to resource constraints. Although, the overall government contribution has been increasing throughout the plan periods, it has not kept pace with the rapid rise in enrolment and escalation in prices. Often inadequacy of financial resources leads to poor infrastructure and physical facilities, low investment in research and development, having adverse impact on the quality of the higher education system.

In order to overcome these problems:

1. The government should increase the public expenditure to a reasonable level.
2. The participation of private sector should be encouraged with regulation.
3. Necessary control and monitoring mechanism must be developed to ensure quality education at reasonable cost.
4 Universities should also open their campuses abroad or tie up with universities and institutions to offer their programmes for mobilizing funds and providing education in the countries where such education is in demand.
5. Encouraging private donations and endowments, strengthening community participation and establishing industry-university linkages from which both the universities and the industrial sector benefit.
6. Universities and colleges can take up research projects from the industries for the generation of funds.
7. Institutes of higher teaching such as IIM, IITs should be increased as per the requirement.

CONCLUSION

India is spending below one per cent of GDP on higher education. Clearly this is inadequate if we aim to transform the knowledge-based economy of India in the 21st Century. The fast growth of the Indian economy, especially in the service sector requires a huge number of employable graduates. Therefore, public expenditure on each segment of the education especially higher education has to increase substantially for further growth of high quality manpower commensurate with India's growing position in the world economy and the urgent need to keep pace with global development in all spheres of science and technology. And to achieve the goals of higher education, the government should invite support from the private sector and generate funds from other sources.

References

Thakare, Dilip, "Budget 2006: Lip Service to Education", *Educational World*, April 2006, pp. 30-35

Bhan, Sonia, "India: Private Sector Energies In Higher Education", www.wes.org

Patil, V.T., "Higher Education in India", www.hinduonnet.com

Tilak, J.B.G., "Privatization of Higher Education", www.bc.edu.com

Index